Language
On A Leash

by Bruce O. Boston

Editorial Experts, Inc.

Library of Congress Cataloging in Publication Data

Boston, Bruce O.
   Language on a leash.

   1. English language—Usage.   2. English language—
Rhetoric.   I. Title.
PE1460.B58   1988   428   88-24636
ISBN 0-935012-10-9 (pbk.)

Editorial Experts, Inc.
85 S. Bragg Street, Suite 400
Alexandria, VA 22312

For Jean

Table Of Contents

Acknowledgments

These pieces were produced over several years and under the very watchful gaze of a number of different readers, editors, and interlocutors, all of whom conspired to keep the author from creating a body of error that would beggar the imagination if the truth got out. Herewith my public thanks for the private kindnesses and loyal assistance of

♦ Janet Horwitz, Pat Gerkin, and Diana Clayton, who served ably as editorial assistants and production managers;

♦ Mara Adams, Eleanor Johnson, Claire Kincaid, Michele Nathan, Peggy Smith, and Priscilla Taylor, for their ruthless blue pencils, their continuing support, and their occasionally embarrassing questions;

♦ the production staff of Editorial Experts, Inc., who worked hard to make things look as good as we tried to make them sound; and

♦ Margaret Morrison, whose unfailing good humor and word-processing skills saved many a production schedule.

Foreword

by Jefferson D. Bates

Bruce Boston is up to his old tricks—giving rhetoric a good name.

Having a chance to read his LOGO*PHILE[1] essays in book form is certainly convenient. Readers no longer need to wait for the next installment of *The Editorial Eye* to enjoy another of his forays into the nuances and crannies of the English language; they merely have to turn the page. With all this gourmet fare collected in a single volume, we might say that we can have our cake and eat it too. But let's not; because Bruce prefers "new clichés," I'll introduce him to one from Missouri I'm reasonably sure he won't have heard before: This book makes me feel like a mule turned loose in the oat bin.

Language On A Leash is a virtuoso performance; I hereby commend him, for having *catenated* its concepts to achieve *entelechy*. If you don't know what all that means, don't feel bad. I didn't either until I read Bruce's "Playing Mozart on a Ukulele" (pp. 20–22). And while these artful and playful essays aren't exactly comparable to hearing Zubin Mehta "play" an orchestra (the enjoyment they give is actually more like listening to the late Glenn Gould's performance of "The Well-Tempered Klavier"), they're not too shabby either.

Where else could one learn not only about the *millihelen*, but also about such other wondrous words as *asyndeton* and *propaedeutic*? And how enlightening it is to find that almost anyone can aspire to being *licentious*, perhaps even *lascivious*, but only a select few can qualify for *lecherous*.

From lechery, it's just a short jump to jealousy. Bruce usually writes with passion and sometimes with eloquence about many aspects of language and usage that concern me deeply. What rankles is his annoying habit of doing it in a way that sometimes makes me wonder why I keep on bothering. Except, of course, when he expresses wrong-headed opinions markedly different from my own.

---

[1] The majority were published as THE LOGO*PHILE, a continuing column written by the author for *The Editorial Eye*, a monthly newsletter for publications professionals, published by Editorial Experts, Inc.

For example? Well, there aren't many, but here's one (page 48) that really raised my blood pressure:

Editors prospecting for and nurturing writing talent should also instruct new writers in the art of writing with cadence. (Technical writing is an exception.)

With that gratuitous parenthetical afterthought, Bruce *grandly* dismisses technical writing as being beyond the pale. As the old saw goes, now he's meddling. Admittedly I'm prejudiced: I had the privilege of apprenticing at the craft of technical writing—and it *is* a craft—under a master teacher. The late Mazie Rodgers Worcester was as concerned about cadence, grace, and style as any writer I've ever known. She cantankerously taught me more about writing with accuracy and clarity (with *precision*, if you will) than I had learned in years of studying—and teaching—conventional English Comp courses.

Bruce admires the essays of Dr. Lewis Thomas, but I suspect he doesn't think of that master stylist as a technical writer. Nevertheless, that's what Dr. Thomas is, and an extraordinarily good one. And he's far from being alone. Other past and present masters of the craft include Robert Ardrey, Isaac Asimov, Paul Davies, Albert Einstein, Martin Gardner, Douglas R. Hofstadter, James R. Newman, and others too numerous to mention.

Even then he usually writes convincingly enough to trigger the anxiety that he might convert me in my old age. He's a dangerous man to have around.

Sometimes, Bruce makes me feel like getting an injunction: He makes things too tough on his fellow writers. Imagine the shock to the nervous system of finding that I have been guilty of committing *pleonasms* all these years. There may be hope for you, but I fear it's too late for me to repent of that particular sin now.

In the end, I think one of the nicest things I can say about this book is that it brought to mind a critic who once remarked that there are only seven (or ten, or however many) writers in the world who can turn out a decent English sentence. Stuff and nonsense. Whatever number he may have ventured, I know of at least one more. His name is Bruce Boston.

Jefferson D. Bates
Reston, Va.
August 1988

Introduction

The fact that these essays have already appeared elsewhere[1] raises a question: Why commit the immodesty of publishing them again? Leaving aside the given that anyone who publishes a column believes that what he thinks is worth saying in print, there are two reasons for bringing out this book.

First, since 1983 there has been a considerable expansion and turnover in the readership of *The Editorial Eye*, where most of these essays first appeared. The turnover has created a completely new audience for many—probably most— of these pieces. And if prior interest is indicative, then the immodesty of reissuing them may yet be balanced by some modest service to a new group of readers.

Second, beyond that group, there is now a much wider readership for matters related to English. A major preoccupation with writing, language, and usage has taken root in our magazines, newspapers, journals, and other media. Not with literature, which is another matter altogether, but with our *language,* which has come to be viewed as a kind of eccentric but beloved relative, about whose well-being everyone in the family is entitled to an opinion. A cottage industry of books on usage has sprung up. Letters-to-the-editor columns gleefully pounce on grammatical howlers, editing errors, and the like. Newsletters run departments that point out their own and others' mistakes. The column from which these pieces were drawn has been a part of that discussion.

Most of the discussants have taken their places along a spectrum anchored at either end by a point of view, stated in the extreme, which says (1) The language is going to hell and the end of Western civilization as we know it is at hand if one more person uses continually to mean *continuously;*[2] and (2) Too many self-appointed busybodies are worried about things that don't matter all that much (except to them). There are "grammatical errors" in Shakespeare,

---

[1] Most appeared between 1983 and 1988 in *The Editorial Eye.* Others were published separately in other publications.

[2] *Continually* means "again and again" or "repeatedly." Continuously means "without interruption or stopping." An airport warning light blinks continually; a river flows continuously.

Milton, and Dryden, so why get uptight? Language changes; therefore, get happy and go with the flow.

Much to my delight, a rereading of the essays presented here reveals a fairly consistent perspective that avoids both these stereotypes. When it comes to English, I think of myself—as these pieces show—neither as one who tries to keep our language cooped up behind impossibly high fences nor as one who lets it run loose, like a neglected and undisciplined hound. The point of view in these essays is that those who care about English, i.e., people who believe clear thinking and felicity of expression matter, aren't required to sign up for either Group 1 or Group 2. Instead, what we ought to do is keep the language on a long but well-anchored leash. "Correct grammar and usage" and "good writing" do not get that way because clear thought and felicity of expression are automatically produced by obedience to absolute rules. They get that way (talent aside) because the only way to keep the tremendous energy of English from dissipating itself in the nebulous jargon of bureaucratese or in any one of a multitude of piecemeal assaults on its integrity is to tether it to the end of a very stout rope.

An analogy. Musicians write and play their music in keys, tempos, and harmonies. When someone slips the leash and wanders off the musical reservation as it is currently mapped out (Schönberg comes to mind; Joyce would be an analogue in literature, Picasso in painting), that act can only be called legitimate or creative in reference to the canons of art that are already there; in fact, it is (curiously) the leash itself that imparts power to the act of escape.

In the matter of English, then, I have come to think of myself as holding one end of a leash, at the other end of which is a language barking its head off, trying to tear off in every which direction, in search of some new way to articulate the meanings all of us depend on. The task is to keep on paying out the leash and pulling it back in whenever the new territory is explored, while considering whether the territory beyond the end of the leash will be worth living in.

In the end, if the English language matters to you, as it does to me, it matters because it is the avatar of thought; it is the way we know the world and are known in it. It is how we manufacture meanings. We cannot think, hope, intend, or believe without it. And as long as, in the words of Saul Bellow, "[there is] an immense, painful longing for a broader, more flexible, fuller, more coherent, more comprehensive account of what we human beings are, who we are, and what this life is for,"[3] keeping it on the leash will matter, too.

Bruce O. Boston
Reston, Va.
August 1988

---

[3] On accepting the Nobel Prize for Literature, December 12, 1976.

I.
The Matter Of English

"Postings on the Refrigerator Door"

ccording to Jim Quinn, the refusal to judge English usage is the basis for all contemporary study of the language, "which has long since concluded that, if you are a native-born speaker of English, you never make a mistake in grammar because you don't know how: grammar is what you say."

This amazing statement appears on page 11 of Quinn's *American Tongue and Cheek* (New York: Penguin, 1982). Quinn's book is billed as a "populist guide to our language"; it reads like a tongue-lashing of the "pop grammarians," among whom Quinn numbers not only Edwin Newman, John Simon, Theodore Bernstein, and William Safire, but also Wilson Follett, Eric Partridge, and H.W. Fowler! On the grounds that Quinn's point of view and research methods constitute a direct attack on what most editors stand for, it deserves a critical look.

The idea that native speakers cannot err, though astonishing to many, is not new. Quinn is quite right that it lies close to the center of the entire discipline of modern linguistics. I believe he is wrong to insist that grammar is only a map of possible utterances in a language. It is also a guide to the standards that enable us to discriminate how well utterances communicate meanings. If grammar is merely what we say, then grammar becomes a tautology, coterminous with its subject, and disappears entirely.

Grammar

If it is anything, grammar is a set of ordering principles, as the medieval curriculum recognized when it grouped grammar with logic and rhetoric to form the basis for the study of all knowledge. If, as Quinn seems to think, grammar is purely descriptive and should not be used prescriptively, then how are we to trust the relationship that language constructs between the reality we experience and how well we communicate that reality? Against what do we measure utterances to make sure they are language and

2

not nonsense? How do we know that "I do my work" is a better sentence than "I does my work," even though many native speakers would use such a sentence and be perfectly well understood? The word *language*, if it means anything at all, carries with it the idea of a commonly agreed upon process of creating meaning, ordered by commonly agreed upon rules.

Because language is a human invention for ordering reality and communicating about it, you cannot abandon that order without eventually paying a price for it, usually in the form of garbled communication and mangled meanings. At a slightly more complex level, you cannot use plural verbs with singular subjects because if you do, you violate a consensus about the logical relationship between language and reality. Languages have singulars and plurals because reality comes at us that way, and we have to have some way of dealing with that fact.

Change

Quinn himself, in mounting his argument, follows closely the basic premise his argument denies. He uses words and puts them in relation to each other according to long-established conventions. If he didn't he would not be understood. More to the point, his book would not have been published. But he is quite right in reminding us that these are conventions, and that conventions change. The real issues are change, rates of change, who decides what changes are acceptable, and which changes threaten the superstructure that holds language in place for all of us.

For better or for worse, the commonly agreed upon answers to those questions lie largely in the hands of the people most of us believe are best at using language. If you want to find out the best way to hit a baseball, you ask someone like George Brett or Don Mattingly. If you want to find out the difference between *flout* and *flaunt*, you ask someone like H.W. Fowler. The fact that Brett and Mattingly are going to disagree on some of the fine points of hitting ought not stop us from soliciting their advice. Nor should the fact that each strikes out occasionally. The fact that "average speakers" do not always agree in their speech with usage authorities and prescriptive grammars is not an argument for abandoning standards.

Much of Quinn's book is given to tongue-clucking over questions that usage authorities tend to be pedantically adamant about, that is, the book goes to the level where change is most vigorously debated. Here we encounter such usage questions as whether *between you and I* is acceptable, whether *gift* is a verb, the "real" meaning of *fulsome*, whether you can use *over* to mean *more than*, and the like. Here he inveighs against the "pop grammarians" for their prescriptiveness. In every instance his approach is to select citations from the *Oxford English Dictionary* showing either that some great writer used the word in question in exactly the sense now frowned upon by some "pop grammarian," or that the usage he himself is championing was in use in centuries past. When Babe Ruth hit a home run, he did not follow the method advocated by George Brett or Don Mattingly. Big deal.

Research Method

Quinn's research method reminds me of nothing so much as the nine-year-old who discovers that *ain't* is in the dictionary and proceeds to pepper his speech with it for a week, to the consternation of his maiden aunts. Quinn's recommendations amount to a kind of linguistic "flashing," testing to see if someone will call the police. And if someone should, Quinn's likely defense would probably be to whip out a 3x5 card that would say something like "While at Oxford, John Milton once mooned one of his professors."

Even college sophomores know that the appearance of something in print is not an argument for its truth or repetition. The same difficulty develops in theological circles, where proving points by quoting isolated verses of Scripture (proof-texting) has been a discredited form of argumentation for a very long time. The point is not that we ought to be able to say *between you and I* because the locution appears in *The Merchant of Venice* (III.ii.321). The point is that good writing and correct speech use the objective case for personal pronouns where it is called for, and that trespassing the boundaries of standard grammar and usage should only be done for good reason. These border crossings are not an argument for a different norm; in fact, they reinforce the norm precisely because they are seen as violations.

Good usage is decided by good writers and by people who take the trouble to learn how to use language well. And that "well" is all-important because it implies standards. Good language is like good art. An artist takes the trouble to learn how to use the tools of color, light, line, and perspective. Good writers get into print; good artists get into galleries and museums. For Quinn, art might as well be the first-grade scrawls of a child on the refrigerator door. But they don't become art because they've been hung.

4

Orwell on Politics and Language*

hat year" is upon us. The cultural and political mavens have unleashed a barrage of commentary, firing in Orwell's direction ("Orwell was wrong") as well as at their own favorite targets ("Orwell was talking about you"), reminding all within earshot of "what Orwell really meant" and cautioning readers that, although Big Brother may not have arrived, Doublethink and Newspeak have. As a metaphor, "1984" has been reduced to a cliché; its very abuse has become an example of the muddled thinking that Orwell tried to unmask. These days, speakers and writers feel entitled to throw "1984" at whatever they happen to dislike, from network TV to telephone answering machines.

But professional writers and editors have to be more discriminating. Our legacy from Orwell is neither debased sociology nor muzzy political analysis. The flame we are bound to keep alive is not the blazing torch of prophecy but the steady glow of quality in the written word. Thus, we need to remind ourselves that, regardless of his accuracy as a prognosticator, George Orwell was among the finest English essayists of this (or any) century. And that is why our required reading this year should be not *1984*, but his essay—now a classic—"Politics and the English Language."

In nearly five decades, this masterpiece has not lost its power to satisfy and sting. It is filled with so many aids for recognizing sins of omission and commission that, if there were a penitential season for writers and editors, this essay could easily become part of the liturgy. Throughout, Orwell is concerned with combating the "half-conscious belief that language is a natural growth...." What language is, he says, is "an instrument which we shape for our own purposes."

Author's Note: When 1984 rolled around, it seemed a good time to remind readers that George Orwell was at least as good a writer as he was prognosticator, and probably better.

That statement, of course, is both the good news and the bad, because language and thought interact. Language "becomes ugly and inaccurate because our thoughts are foolish," he says, "but the slovenliness of our language makes it easier for us to have foolish thoughts." He argues that the two most common writing problems—those with the highest potential for foolishness—are staleness of imagery and lack of concreteness. Orwell counsels avoiding the following at all costs (his examples are different but the point remains):

♦ Dying metaphors (*bottom line, free lunch, doing your homework*)

♦ The routine interment of verbs (*exhibit a tendency to, under the direction of, make mention of*)

♦ Pretentious words (*effectuate, ineluctable, Weltanschauung*)

♦ Meaningless words (one of Orwell's examples, from a poetry critic, is superb: "Comfort's catholicity of perception and image, strangely Whitmanesque in range...continues to evoke that trembling atmospheric accumulative hinting at a cruel and inexorably serene timelessness....")

As aids to concreteness, Orwell offers six rules. I commend them to every editor and writer in 1984 (indeed, in any year); they fit quite nicely on a 4x6 file card, suitable for tacking above the desk at eye level:

1. Never use a metaphor, simile, or other figure of speech which you are used to seeing in print.
2. Never use a long word where a short one will do.
3. If it is possible to cut a word out, always cut it out.
4. Never use the passive where you can use the active.
5. Never use a foreign phrase, a scientific word, or a jargon word if you can think of an everyday English equivalent.
6. Break any of these rules sooner than say anything outright barbarous.

The common sense tucked away in the last of these sets Orwell apart. He recognized that, although his rules were elementary, their adoption required something akin to a religious conversion. He was also aware that there would be not only much backsliding but also much worshiping of false gods. Writers need to beware the ritualistic avoidance of the passive and the mechanistic reductionism of readability formulas. Slavish adherence to rules like these results in the death of style. For their part, editors should never forget that style sheets are conventions, not commandments. They do not so much define orthodoxy as defend against heresy.

As the Orwell revival gets underway, writers and editors have better credentials than most for participating. We have every right to claim him as our own, and to admire and learn from his penetration into the profound relationships between our times and the fragile web of words we use to announce and describe them.

Minority Report

am getting worried about the "Short and Simple Vigilantes (SSVs)." In the last few years they've been out to lynch practically anybody who dared use a word of more than two syllables or construct a compound-complex sentence. Their message is as ubiquitous (a word they would disallow) as it is monotonous. Keep it short, simple, direct, uncomplicated. No jargon. (Jargon is generally defined as a word I use that they don't.) Never use a long word when a short one will do. Use active verbs. Avoid embedded clauses. Take readings on the Fog Index. Write this way.

Before I become the guest of honor at an SSV necktie party, let me say that I believe all of this advice is good, most of the time. Bloviated prose is a millstone around the neck of language; as such, it is probably a threat to civilization itself. A society choking on its own gobbledygook is not a pretty sight, and we all knew some drastic measures were in order.

Miles to Go

An amorphous process of language reform—one hesitates to call it a movement—has been at work for about ten years now, to some good effect. Although the federal bureaucracy promptly ignored President Carter's Executive Order 12044, designed to clean up the government's language, "plain English" laws have been passed in several states and seem to be working. Banks, insurance companies, and lawyers are coming around. And, for all the academic upper lips curled in the direction of the "pop grammarians" (Edwin Newman, William Safire, John Simon, *et al.*), these self-appointed praetorians of the language have elevated the awareness of language and correct usage to a degree unheard of a generation ago. Although much has improved, much remains to be done.

But there is a darker side to all this. It emerges most prominently, I think, in the unquestioned assumption of the SSVs. Their banner is emblazoned with the device of Coleridge: "Whatever is translatable into other and simpler words of the same language, without loss of sense or dignity, is bad." For many years before his death,

Rudolf Flesch was a champion worthy of Coleridge. His *The ABC of Style* (out of print), in many ways a commendable work, regrettably confused too many personal prejudices with the absolute truth. His sensitivity to pomposity unfortunately led him, on occasion, to throw common sense overboard. Many SSVs, following Flesch, seem to think that, although there is nothing wrong with an extensive vocabulary or with dependent clauses, there is something wrong with using them.

Style and Vocabulary

This attitude raises some questions. First, if the SSVs have their way, what becomes of style? Granted, the convoluted style of Henry James is hard to read, but many argue that it is worth the effort. Opacity deserves to be attacked, but if quick and efficient become the preferred stylistic canons, it is a short step to childish, boring, and stupid.

A second question arises in the matter of vocabulary. The SSVs, acting in the name of "the reader," eagerly blue-pencil any word or phrase that strikes them as too long, stuffy, abstract, or arcane; worse, they simply strike down anything (heaven forfend) they aren't familiar with. The reader is whipsawed by the logic of a self-fulfilling prophecy. Because certain words are thought to be beyond the ken of the reader, they are used less and less often. The reader never gets a chance to learn them, and is to that degree impoverished. If, as Flesch has it, *comply with* and *alter* are merely pompous synonyms for *follow* and *change*, and we deliberately avoid the former, isn't something being lost?

Maybe it's time we stopped looking out for readers and left readers to look out for themselves. Sometime during the last 30 years, something strange and terrible happened. It used to be that readers had a responsibility to improve their vocabularies by looking up unfamiliar words. Today it is the writer's responsibility to avoid any word any reader might not be familiar with—even if it is the right word. This is wrong.

While striving to keep our prose lean and mean, let's not forget that nuance is the soul of any language. There, writers can seek their full powers of expression. Power of expression, in turn, is absolutely necessary to power of thought. By any standard, English is one of the most powerful, most expressive languages that has yet evolved. If we sacrifice that power on the altar of the SSVs, we've lost something of incomparable value.

"Close Enough Is Not Good Enough"

riters and editors are warriors. They are warriors against the attitude toward language that says, "close enough is good enough."

I am continually amazed and puzzled at how tenacious that attitude is. I encounter it most frequently—but by no means exclusively—among high school and college students, many of whom have a concern for language that vacillates between ennui and contempt. (I have nearly abandoned hope for any felicity of expression. I would settle for the next step beyond the endless iteration of "I mean, like....").

I have put my puzzlement to one of the resident teenagers: "9 x 7 is 63, and 62.95 is not acceptable, right? Close enough is not good enough."

"Right," says he.

"Then why are you willing to speak, with your own mouth, a sentence like 'Them books are mine' when you know perfectly well that you should use 'those'?"

His answer is, "You understand me, right? Then why do I have to be grammatically correct?"

My rejoinder, to the effect that he is not fulfilling his duty to make himself understood, but is relying on me to do his job, meets with a jaunty "Don't sweat it, Dad, it's no big thing."

General Orders

It's about time someone declared war; remember you read about it here first. Writers, editors, and, yes, English teachers, gather 'round the flag! Our battle cry is, "Close Enough Is Not Good Enough!" Throw open the window, à la Peter Finch in the movie *Network*, and shout it out to anyone within earshot.

Shout, but don't forget that we are not going to win by decibels alone. We need a battle plan. And we have one. There are plenty of good reasons why it's better to write and speak correctly. Our secret weapon is that good English is good for you and will get you more than bad English will in the long run. Thus, in this war, the objective is not to dominate by conquest but to tempt and, at last, to seduce. Here are a few carrots to dangle in front of the donkey of your choice.

1. Using good English automatically makes its users more courteous, and courtesy begets more than rudeness. Using correct writing and speech does not require others to divine meanings from syntactical entrails. There is social value in being recognized as a thoughtful person who never uses the wrong pronominal case and seldom splits an infinitive. Good English can even prompt invitations to lots of nice places; poor language (like bad language) can get you not invited back. And a well-timed bread and butter letter might just land that job.

2. Good English saves time. Imprecision and error go hand in hand with circumlocution and the necessity to revise and correct, sooner or later. The warrior can, insidiously, encourage time-saving by never supplying the right word nor filling in the gaps for others. Profess stupidity about the meaning of run-on sentences. These minor acts of rebellion on your part will lead, sooner or later, to more precision and expanded vocabularies; it happens a lot sooner than you would think, believe me.

3. Good English saves space. Politicians whose biographies are full of phrases like "hopes and aspirations" and actress-authors who natter on about their "deeply profound experiences" in Tibetan lamaseries are merely using up good paper. Warriors should tell them how much more they could say about themselves if they would only learn to prune their pleonasms. "'Hopes' will do" " 'Profound' will do" are appropriate sallies in such contexts, if you don't mind dirty looks.

4. Good English develops discipline and a superior sense of order, which are better by a long shot than a flaccid will and rampant disorganization. Spelling, punctuation, grammar, and usage are all tools, and respect for tools is the first law of any craft. Warriors are allowed to riposte with a paraphrase of Ben Franklin: "Keep thy tools and thy tools will keep thee."

5. Most of the time, using good English takes no more effort than using bad English. Most of the students of my acquaintance, for instance, know perfectly well the rules about using "Mary

and I went to the game" instead of "Me and Mary..."; they use the latter construction simply out of habit. The quickest way for warriors to change bad habits is by not reinforcing them. Don't respond to such sentences.

6. Good English fosters a craftsmanlike attitude. There were master woodcarvers in medieval Europe who spent entire lifetimes carving the undersides of choir seats. In writing and speaking, what is unseen is often more important than what is seen; bad writing is never beautiful. Here, warriors may take the high road and talk about art or utility; probe for the line of least resistance.

7. Good English increases the range of meaning available for the writer to play with. Language without nuance is like a one-color rainbow...bland, tasteless, dull, insipid, commonplace, routine, jejune, prosaic, humdrum, quotidian, nondescript, unappetizing, and just plain blah. This is an area where subtlety is rewarded: Serve unsalted food and lukewarm beverages as a sneak attack.

8. Good English fosters clear thinking. Writers and editors know that nothing is better at forcing someone to think through something than having to write it down. "Y'know" simply doesn't cut it when it comes to even the most elementary acts of explication, explanation, and persuasion. The warrior's correct response to "y'know" is "No, I don't. Tell me about it."

Writers, editors, English teachers, unite! We have nothing to use but our brains! To arms! *Aux barricades*! They shall not pass! Take no prisoners! Close enough is not good enough!

Gleanings, or, Obiter Dicta

n *obiter dictum* (pl. *dicta*) is an incidental remark, a thing said "by the way." As a literary device, the *obiter dictum* is a convenient way for the writer (more properly, the conversationalist) to pass along ideas that seemed particularly interesting, worthy of the attention and perhaps the reflection of friends. Sometimes the *obiter dictum* is an inadvertence; other times (as with the studied aphorisms of Logan Pearsall Smith) it betrays an eye-squinting effort. Many working editors develop files of these gleanings—quotes, clips, paragraphs, articles, poems, graphs, jokes, chapters. They are the kernels of grain that remain behind when each day's portion of reading is harvested.

The trouble is, for the most part, these gleanings remain in the garner, seldom to be seen again, although one of the best collections has been published by Herbert R. Mayes, as *An Editor's Treasury* (two vols., New York: Atheneum, 1968). Gleanings get buried because today's agenda tends to overwhelm yesterday's resolve to share the nourishment of the written word.

No more. My theory is that your files might just as well be as cluttered as mine. Here, then, are a few *obiter dicta* from my files. No particular selection criterion has been applied, other than that they all have something to do with our common labors. Plant them in your own field.

♦ *On the necessity of language.* "Anybody who thinks that men invented language as they have invented...buttons or coins or stamps is certainly incapable of understanding one word of the history of mankind. Words are not our tools; since Adam first called things good and evil men have cried, spoken, shrieked, screamed, sung, called, and commanded because they must, not because they would. True language is an expression of necessity, not a tool in man's hand."

—Eugen Rosenstock-Huessy

♦ *On wordiness.* "In language, as in mathematics, the shortest distance between two points is a straight line."

—*Lois DeBakey*

♦ *On the debasement of language.* "One of the greatest mischiefs which confront us today is the growing debasement of language, on the one hand vulgarized and on the other corrupted with a particularly odious academic jargon. This is dangerous. A civilization which loses its power over its own language has lost its power over the instrument by which it thinks. Without some power, there is neither greatness nor accuracy of thought."

—*Henry Beston*

♦ *On editing.* "Editors sit between the virgin manuscript and the public. We are the first real reader the book is exposed to, and like a kindly parent, we are the first to say, 'Your slip is showing.'"

—*Olga Litowinsky*

♦ *On jargon.* "The danger of jargon is that by using it we delude ourselves into thinking that the showhorses of terminology are the workhorses of thinking. The final form of that delusion is reification, 'thingifying' all the abstractions we pile onto each other, until at last we subtly convince ourselves that the word and what the word signifies are one."

—*Richard A. Lanham*

♦ *On words.* "Words are like prescription lenses; they obscure what they do not make clear."

—*Stefan Kanfer*

♦ *On language, responsibility, and life.* "'In the beginning was the Word,' as St. John wrote in his Gospel, and he was right. The word is the beginning of consciousness, for the race of man and for every individual in it, and as the arrangement of words grows into a system of language so does consciousness develop and grow. Language is also the beginning of responsibility, a word whose Latin root means to respond (answer, justify, defend). Without language we can react like the beasts and the fishes; with it we can respond like men and women, responsibly. One of the things we are responsible for is language itself, next to life our most precious possession."

—*William McPherson*

Rhetorical Revival

hetoric has fallen on hard times; as a result the grace of public speech has too long suffered. When *rhetoric* is used, most people think of something like "overblown speechifying"; rhetoric has come to mean the babble of people who have little of interest or significance to say, whether in speech or in print. It is a scandal of our time that the most common modifier for rhetoric is *mere*.

When the Greeks first got interested in rhetoric, they took human speech with a seriousness that was as bracing as it was good for civic health. For them it was both an art (expressive speech) and a science (of persuasion). In the classical tradition, rhetoric was the light that made thoughts shine. Socrates, Plato, and Aristotle theorized about it. Romans like Cicero and Quintillian developed and shaped rhetoric so that it became an indispensable part of the medieval curricular *trivium*—grammar, logic, and rhetoric—then considered to be the foundation for all useful knowledge (a pretty good pedagogy for that time or any, considering the human propensity for slovenliness in both language and reasoning).

More recently, during the 19th century, instruction in rhetoric became less systematic, backing away from the highly theoretical approach devised by classical and medieval authors. The emphasis shifted from one strong strain in the rhetorical tradition, which favored forcefully expressed arguments, to another strain that favored showy display and a more stylistic use of language—put more crudely, from the steak to the sizzle. A famous case in point is the acclaim heaped on Edward Everett's tediously mediocre oration at Gettysburg and the lukewarm response given Lincoln's rhetorical jewel.

In recent decades, the increasing synonymy of rhetoric with the babblings of political blowhards has blackened the reputation of rhetoric considerably. But a countertrend is afoot and its positive signs should be encouraged. Chief among the positives is the emergence of a few good public speakers among politicians themselves (e.g., Edward Kennedy, Mario Cuomo, Ronald Reagan, Pierre du Pont, Jesse Jackson). These powerful speakers, like Martin

Luther King, Jr., and John F. Kennedy in a previous generation, are beginning to give rhetoric a good name.

Another encouraging development is that more and more corporate executives are relying on professional wordsmiths to craft their speeches, which at least elevates the expression of substance in business communication, if not always its delivery. There is also good news in the revived interest in "communication skills," written and oral, as evidenced in the explosion of books and newsletters, the abundance of workshops and seminars, and the burgeoning cottage industry of "communication consultants" who are making a good living by advising people on what (when you look at it closely) amounts to their rhetoric. And finally, *mirabile dictu*, colleges are teaching rhetoric again and calling it that.

All this is encouraging to a middle-aged practitioner. For those of us who have kept the faith, rhetoric properly understood and skillfully practiced has always had the potential to put the other predominant form of public discourse, advertising, on the defensive—where it belongs. For us, keeping the faith has always meant that rhetoric would make its comeback because it is essential. And it is essential not only because all communication should be clear, forceful, and in the end persuasive, but also because a self-governing people require reasoned and articulate argument as a matter of self-preservation.

So, let's stop bad-mouthing rhetoric and start renewing our acquaintance with and deepening our commitment to that ancient art. We may find in it not only better understanding, but our better selves.

Huxley Was Right

hen 1984 rolled around, much ink was spilled over George Orwell's dark vision and whether we had at last arrived at the cultural dead end he foresaw. Neil Postman, in his inquiry into the impact of television on public discourse, *Amusing Ourselves to Death* (New York: Viking, 1985), argues that anyone distracted by Orwell apocalyptic's language has missed the point: It was Aldous Huxley we should have been listening to all along.

Postman's essay is one of the most insightful cultural critiques I have read since the late sixties and early seventies, when that kind of book was a minor industry. Everyone who cares about language and the profound relationship between the written word and rational thought must, not should but must, read this book.

A Compelling Thesis

Postman's thesis is easy to understand and brilliantly argued: Television has drastically altered the very nature (not just the means) of public discourse. Public discussion of serious issues—his word is "exposition"—was once predominant in American society. But since the electronic age has enabled us to transmit both information and image at the speed of light, the inevitable has occurred. Impressions have overpowered thoughts and our experience of the world has been profoundly falsified by the values that accompany television.

Television news programming, for example, requires a kind of minimalism: Every event must be stripped of its context. But context embodies the meanings that enable us to understand events fully. To succeed as a medium, television must supplant reflection, explication, and explanation with amusement and entertainment. (After all, who will sit and *watch* some scholar think and talk about what it all means when they can watch it all *happen* on "Eyewitness News.")

Thus, substance and logic are no longer the raw material for the public's decisions about anything; these have been replaced by gestures, symbols, and images. Fewer and fewer Americans have thoughts about what happens around them; instead, they have opinions. Politics, news, religion, education, and commerce— among the most basic forms of human intercourse and thus human discourse—have succumbed to the siren of the TV screen. Public discourse, understood as the deliberate, well-reasoned argument, has been replaced. Every fact must be transformed into a drama. Every nuance must be eliminated. Every complex issue must be reduced to the subtlety of the simplest dichotomy (yes/no, we/they, good/evil, right/wrong). And it's not merely that "L.A. Law" gets ratings that a lecture on the justice system would not. Pacing always outdraws pondering, whether we're talking about political commercials that sell a candidate's image instead of his views; a 45-second news clip (with accompanying analysis) from Panama; a Billy Graham rally, in which God is delivered on cue, in time for the next commercial; "Sesame Street," the classroom for millions in which no student can ask a question; or the 15-second solution to the mindless domestic crisis of waxy buildup. Television has slowly eroded both the forms and the skills of reflection and thoughtfulness; worse, it has transformed public discourse, of necessity, into a form of entertainment.

A Metaphor

The metaphor in Postman's title arises from the basic differences between *1984* (San Diego, CA: Harcourt Brace Jovanovich, Inc., 1983) and *Brave New World* (New York: Harper & Row, 1987). In Orwell's book, the danger to culture was oppression; in Huxley's, the threat was much more insidious: Our minds would eventually be narcotized by pleasure and the culture would die of its own distractions. In Huxley's vision, people were increasingly diverted by entertainments, with the resultant loss of mental discipline. Orwell's nightmare was thought control; Huxley's was the disappearance of the need for thinking. According to *Brave New World*, the human spirit is more likely to be devastated by a Happy Face than by the brooding countenance of Big Brother.

A Lesson for Editors

For those of us who earn our daily bread wrestling with print media, Postman's analysis is chilling. Paraphrasing Shakespeare, he wonders "who is prepared to take arms against a sea of amusements?" A basic problem, of course, is getting a hearing for his very unamusing argument. Not everyone believes that TV is a problem. Even more depressing, he admits that there is probably no cure for the malaise he describes.

Because the problem lies not *in what* we watch, but *that* we watch, Postman suggests that a solution may lie somewhere in the direction of changing *how* we watch. A basic hindrance in getting at that issue, however, is our lack of understanding about the true nature of television and its relationship to information and reason. Says Postman, we need to ask ourselves about the moral biases of all forms of information transmittal. More narrowly, we must ask what meaning TV gives to such terms as *piety*, *patriotism*, *privacy*, *judgment*, and *understanding*. "To ask," says Postman, "is to break the spell." Another possibility, he says, is a concerted effort to lay to rest the myth that no ideology accompanies technology. All technology, he insists, comes equipped with a program for social change simply because it construes reality; it is neither a neutral force nor always a friend to culture. To ignore these facts is to become their victim.

In the end, Postman suggests, we may be able to do no better than to follow the example of Huxley himself. Sharing the belief of H.G. Wells that "human history is a race between education and disaster," Huxley wrote continually about the necessity of understanding both the politics and the "way of knowing" embedded in all media. For writers and editors, that means constantly reinforcing the power of language to disenchant the myths created by television the medium. Which means we must never surrender in our fight to gain a hearing. Above all, it means we must never stop believing that what we see on the screen is, in a fundamental way, false.

Playing Mozart on a Ukulele

riters, and to a lesser degree editors, are increasingly flagellated by proponents of clear expression to excise uncommon words from manuscripts. The argument against unusual words is most often advanced in the name of "not turning off the reader"; by now it has become the loudest chorus in the Clear Communications repertoire.

The logic of it all is depressingly simple: If you use a word a reader doesn't know, the reader may trip, stumble, or fall. The reader will then get upset and flip the page or close the book. Not only that (Horrors!), using unusual words is *pedantic*! Prose should be as proletarian as possible.

The most vigorous proponent of this point of view was the late Rudolf Flesch, whose *The ABC of Style* (out of print) and *The Art of Readable Writing* (New York: Macmillan, 1986) have had a widespread impact on writers and editors. His work (as well as that of boon companions such as Robert Gunning) is full of advice on substituting plainer, shorter words for longer, more complicated ones. Some of this has been all to the good, but some of it has been just plain silly. To take one quick example among scores that could be chosen: *The ABC of Style* says that "Thank you for your cooperation" is "stiff," whereas "Thank you for helping us" is "better." The fact that *cooperation* and *help* don't mean the same thing is bypassed entirely.

I find it comforting that the people least swayed by this kind of thinking are people who write well. Admittedly, there is (for some) some linguistic ostentation in summoning up a word like *propaedeutic* when one means "introductory instruction," but that is not all there is to it.

That's why *The Oxter English Dictionary* by George Stone Saussy III (New York: Facts on File Publications, 1984) is worth reading: *Oxter* is an English dialect word derived from the Latin, *axilla*, meaning armpit. This is truly a wonderful work. It presents and defines unusual words, and offers quotations that use the words in context. The quotations alone are priceless. Saussy's is a labor of love: He is not a professional lexicographer, but simply someone interested enough in the richness of English to spend the time it takes to track words down. The fact that a large proportion of the words do not appear in standard dictionaries makes his achievement the more remarkable.

One of the best parts of *Oxter* is the testimony enlisted in support of Saussy's basic thesis. All of it wisely points to semantic versatility not as a basis of literary merit but as language's basic business: meaning itself. In other words, there's nothing wrong with using any word, as long as it's the right one.

One could begin building the case for unusual words with a quote from James Gould Cozzens, who, when *By Love Possessed* (San Diego, CA: Harcourt Brace Jovanovich, 1957) was attacked for its difficult vocabulary, noted that "sometimes the long word will be the right word and I don't scruple to use it—if the reader doesn't know it, it's time he learned." Robert Nye wrote to tell Saussy:

> I love and respect the English language and have always sought to use it as carefully as possible. If this causes me to use an unusual word...it is because the unusual word more exactly expresses what I am trying to say.

Alexander Theroux's comment on the book's premise is certainly the most trenchant and perhaps the best:

> People mistakenly believe, through stupidity or sloth, that a "big word" is used by writers in pretentious excuse for showing-off, when the fact is, for anyone who takes his work seriously, such words are not used to obfuscate but to clarify. A given word is neither pompous nor plain when you come right down to it, but a person is either educated or un-. As far as neologisms [are concerned], it is no different than a painter mixing a new and better color in order to express something or other more accurately.

For logophiles, *Oxter* is the equivalent of a lifetime supply of M&Ms ® : Its entries melt in your mouth. Who could forbear reaching for a treat like *entelechy*, the one word that expresses the complete realization of a concept? Or *catenate*, to express the idea of linking things together, chainlike? Or (a personal favorite) the *millihelen*, a unit of measure for beauty (on the premise that it took the face of one whole Helen to launch a thousand ships)?

One could scarcely make a case of the proposition that the vocabulary of English is contracting; it clearly is not. Why, then, make the effort to preserve such linguistic oddments and scraps? What's the difference, so long as the message is understood by the widest possible audience? The difference is the same as that between the few basic chords any Waikiki beach boy can play on a ukulele and what Zubin Mehta achieves when he "plays" a great orchestra. You may not be tempted to sing along with Mehta, but, on the other hand, have you ever tried to play Mozart on a ukulele?

Cultural Literacy and "Editing Down"

ust in case you've been off doing a guest editorship at the *Bora-Bora Bulletin of Polynesian Studies*, you probably need an update on the recent op ed dustup. We're talking "cultural literacy" here, folks, and it's not a pretty sight.

The term was devised by Professor E.D. Hirsch, Jr., of the University of Virginia, and it serves as the title for his national best seller *Cultural Literacy: What Every American Needs to Know*. (Boston: Houghton-Mifflin, 1987). His thesis is that cultural literacy (defined as the "background information" audiences need to understand what is said in books, newspapers, magazines, and other media) is essential to getting along as a citizen, consumer, and worker. To live successfully in the modern world depends on some shared universe of discourse, Hirsch says, and too many people lack the requisite data for it. People who think that Leningrad is a city in Jamaica; or who don't understand the meaning of the terms *inflation, totalitarianism,* or *menopause*; or whose sense of history does not enable them to date the Civil War within half a century lack the ability to understand what they're being told. The book is a serious brief for the recovery of information as a basis for education and life.

Predictably, the book has become the impetus for yet another round of tsk-tsking by colleagues in the editorial profession. More on the editors later.

What has attracted the most attention in Hirsch's book is not his argument about cultural literacy but "the list." An appendix to the book offers about 2,500 terms that the author and fellow compilers believe a culturally literate high school graduate should be able to identify, understand, know, or at least be comfortable in the same room with. (It's not that students necessarily should have learned these things in school. A student might never have been taught the phrase *trial balloon* directly, or might never use it in daily conversation, but he or she should know what it means.) The list includes items from history (*1066, William Penn*), geography (*Mount Rainier, Morocco*), literature (*Shelley, H.G. Wells*), science (*pediatrics, Enrico Fermi*), and so on. The list has prompted lots of arguments on the selection criteria, for example, why Pericles is on it and Pythagoras is not. But that's hardly the point; the list could be longer, shorter, or different. The point is whether it is broadly representative of the American cultural heritage—which it is—not whether it is definitive, which it could never be.

A lot of people have been using the list to keep score, as if having 87 percent of the terms in your cultural vocabulary makes you more cultured than an office mate who got a mere 83 percent. That may be an amusing or embarrassing party game, but it's irrelevant. If Hirsch is right, the problem is that the American people's ability to understand each other and the world they live in is eroding. And that's serious.

But there's more, and it has to do with our own fraternity. According to Oberlin College biology professor Michael Zimmerman, preliminary indications are that editors have nothing to be smug about. We are part of the problem. In a *Washington Post* article ("Editors Are Dummies," January 12, 1988), Zimmerman discussed the results of a nationwide poll he took of "an education-ally elite group": managing editors of newspapers. His purpose was to test how widespread basic scientific ignorance might be among people we have every right to assume have the kind of cultural literacy Hirsch is talking about. Admittedly, Zimmerman's inquiry was limited to science, but the results are disquieting. Here are some of his findings:

♦ Only 51 percent of the sample disagreed strongly with the state-ment "Dinosaurs and humans lived contemporaneously."

♦ A full one-third did not disagree strongly with the statement "The earth is approximately 6,000 to 20,000 years old."

♦ Only 41 percent disagreed strongly with the statement "Adam and Eve were actual people," and only 57 percent disagreed strongly that "every word in the Bible is true."

The list goes on. Zimmerman's conclusion is legitimate: "When this 'elite' group retains such an unsophisticated view of science, we can be certain that many other groups are at least as unsophisti-cated." He cites in evidence former Arizona Governor Evan Mecham's hapless aide, who testified before a legislative committee that teachers should not impose their belief that the world is round on students who have been brought up to believe it is flat.

But editors may be part of the problem in another way. I suspect that one of the reasons behind the cultural illiteracy documented by Hirsch and Zimmerman is a kind of condescension, based chiefly on the growing assumption among writers and editors that readers are always more stupid than we can imagine. This assumption leads to the perspective that we should not overtax their brains with (a) historical, scientific, or literary allusions, (b) "technical" terms, (c) unusual words, (d) words with "too many syllables," (e) long sentences, or (f) arguments that require an attention span longer than the time it takes to peel a banana. What such assumptions produce, of course, is a self-fulfilling prophecy. They create the very readership that the likes of Hirsch and Zimmerman bemoan. By "editing down" to readers, we are shaping inelastic minds, just as educators who "dumb down" textbooks are building half-full minds.

Of course, editors shouldn't give up on making documents clearer, simpler, and more readable. But when we are willing to "edit down" because we have lost faith in our readers or because we assume they are not participants in the same culture we are, we make a big mistake. We are slowly but inevitably creating nonreaders, people who finally will be unable to take any joy from drawing on what they know to understand something new—because we are subtly teaching them to draw on less and less. Soon, the well just dries up.

II.
The Writer's Notebook

The Ax, the Pruning Hook, the X-Acto® Knife, and the Metronome

"Writing is easy. All you have to do is cross out the wrong words."
—*Mark Twain*

eter Drucker, the management consultant, has a reputation for calling them the way he sees them. Writers can learn something from Drucker, who refers to his first draft as "the zero draft." His reasoning is that he is entitled to start counting only after he gets something down on paper.

Everyone who writes seriously knows that the real work begins only after there is something to work on. Beginners think to themselves: "If I come up with a great idea, it can carry me." Wrong. Even the noblest of ideas, the most absorbing of themes, can be twisted out of shape in the hands of a careless craftsman; but, in the loving hands of a master like Annie Dillard, even the description of so prosaic a thing as an anthill or a leaf can dazzle.

Good writing is mostly rewriting. Anthony Burgess says he might revise a page as many as 20 times. Short story writer Roald Dahl states that by the time he nears the end of a story, the first part will have been reread and corrected as many as 150 times. If memory serves, Hemingway claimed to have rewritten the final chapter of *A Farewell to Arms* 39 times.

There is nothing particularly praiseworthy in this; it is simply a fact of life for people who care about language, or more to the point, about getting things right. If you want to write, you rewrite. But editing yourself is hard to do, mostly because writers are easily seduced by their own prose. The editorial act must therefore be a deliberate infliction of pain, a conscious and vigorous assent to the

27

proposition well expressed by magazine writer Bil Gilbert: "Writing is essentially weeding out your own stupidity."

A Set of Tools

The Ax

But there are tools that writers can use to improve their work. The first is the ax. It should be laid to the root of entire paragraphs—those that don't belong, that belabor the obvious, or that add just enough detail to distract the reader but not enough to truly illuminate. An entire paragraph can often be distilled into a phrase, or sometimes even a word, which can be added to a preceding or following paragraph. The result is a piece that becomes more taut, and taut is better than slack.

The Pruning Hook

This tool inflicts the most pain, because it is best applied to the turns of phrase we most admire. Disagreeable as it is, writers would do well to follow the advice of novelist Nancy Hale, who counsels excising what seems most clever, most apt, most apposite. Her perfectly sound reasoning is that writers wouldn't admire their own words so much if they weren't protecting them. (No mother believes her baby is ugly!)

The point of pruning writing is the same as for pruning apple trees: Not so much to get rid of the dead branches (which are easy enough to spot) as to shape the tree to produce the best possible fruit. Pruning can involve cutting off live limbs, which may be beautiful in themselves, but bad for the tree in light of its purpose. An unpruned article, like an unpruned tree, wastes its natural energy.

The X-Acto® Knife

This tool is as essential to self-editing as to doing paste-up. Use it to attack the manuscript phrase by phrase and word by word: Is this verb the best possible one? Does this analogy work? Is this metaphor forced? Isn't that phrase really too threadbare to use? As a precision instrument, the X-Acto® knife is well designed for the surgical removal of such minute blemishes as the misplaced comma and the superfluous adverb.

The Metronome

Finally, one of the tools of self-editing most often neglected by even the most careful writers is the metronome. Its job is to measure out the cadence of the writer's words. James J. Kilpatrick recommends in *The Writer's Art* (Kansas City, MO: Andrews, McMeel &

Parker, 1984) that writers who want to master cadence write verse. I concur. This does not mean writing free verse—which Robert Frost once likened to playing tennis with the net down—but verse with rhyme schemes and meter: sonnets, rondeaux, villanelles, haiku. The poetry doesn't have to be good; it just has to be workmanlike. Sound out the sentences. Unless writers want their words to march across the page with all the discipline of the Keystone Kops, they need to pay attention to cadence.

When to Quit?

When does this process end, if at all? Any good piece of writing can be ruined with too much tinkering. But, as Tolstoy observed, "I scarcely ever read my published writings, but if by chance I come across a page, it always strikes me: All this must be rewritten; this is how I should have written it." The real writer is never satisfied because every piece, if it is done right, is still full of potential the moment it is finished.

So, the short answer is that the process never ends; the clock merely runs out, and the time comes to tear the paper from the typewriter and press it into the hands of the next editor. Each piece must be sent off the way the girl back home sends her young soldier off to war, with a heart that longs for just one more day, hour, minute.

Cadence: The Key to Effective Speechwriting

avid Gergen, former presidential speechwriter and director of communications in the Reagan White House, calls speechwriting "an unnatural act." He's right. It is an occupation fit only for masochists, having all the frustrations and problems of "real" writing and none of the rewards. Writers get bylines; speechwriters get anonymity. When the speech goes well, the speaker gets all the credit; when it flops, the speechwriter gets all the blame.

Yet there are rewards. Some are overt. A few top corporate speechwriters earn six-figure salaries; many earn more than $50,000 a year. Sometimes the satisfactions are less tangible but just as real. If you work for a politician who is elected to high office, your words can reach millions. And there are special satisfactions that go with mastering the craft itself.

Writing for the Ear

Writing speeches is a potential minefield for the unprepared writer. Part of the problem is that many newcomers to speechwriting, even though they may be fine writers or editors, know little about the niceties associated with preparing public addresses.

The most critical difference, of course, is that writing for a live audience means writing for the ear. Many a well-formed written sentence falls on the ear like a brick; many fine speeches, when transcribed, read as if they had been written by Morpheus himself.

Guidelines on writing for the ear can be found in the myriad books on speechwriting on the market today. Only a few are worth reading all the way through, but among the more helpful is Dorothy Sarnoff's *Speech Can Change Your Life* (New York: Dell, 1972). (The best texts, of course, are great speeches.) Books on speechwriting offer advice on using familiar words, simple ideas, and short sentences, and avoiding tricky words such as homonyms, words that are hard to pronounce, and double entendres. But most of these books either ignore or gloss over the most helpful element in creating a speech that is easy to listen to and that sticks with the audience: cadence.

Cadence

Cadence is critical to speeches because from it arise audience involvement, force, harmony, dignity, and in truly great speeches, majesty. All languages have distinctive rhythms and cadences when well spoken, and English is no exception. The basic natural rhythm of English is found in the simple declarative sentence. The direct oral style is more appreciated in American English than in French or German, for example.

The most effective cadences in speaking are found in the single direct statement and the simple variations that can be made from it—what I call the double and the triple. Simple statements fall most powerfully on the ear:

"Keep hope alive."—*Jesse L. Jackson*

"I have a dream."—*Martin Luther King, Jr.*

"But let us begin."—*John F. Kennedy*

Simple statements are most effectively used either to introduce a point in a speech or to sum it up. Many speechwriters use simple sentences as a set of bookends for a particular paragraph or as a form of verbal punctuation for several related points. In this latter regard, one of the most effective (though overshadowed) uses of such statements is Martin Luther King's use of "Let freedom ring" in his renowned "I Have a Dream" speech.

There are several kinds of doubles, but they are usually used either to offer a contrast or to provide balance to a sentence. The opening line of Kennedy's inaugural address provides an excellent example:

"We observe today

not a victory of a party, but a celebration of freedom—

symbolizing an end as well as a beginning,

signifying renewal as well as change."

The basic rhythm here is provided by the sets of pairs, which provide both opposition and apposition. Each of the three sets presents a different contrast, but together they compose a satisfying progression to the speaker's theme for the entire speech—America's entry into a new era.

Several structural devices can be used to set up doubles: either...or; neither...nor; not (only) this...but (also) that; if...then.

The double can also be used to contrast ideas and is particularly effective when alliteration can be used to set the contrast off, as in Lincoln's remark: "There can be no successful appeal from the ballot to the bullet; and those who take such an appeal are sure to lose their cause and pay the costs." Here, we have three doubles—a set of balanced clauses, each focusing on an alliterative pair.

John Kennedy was a master at using the rhythm of the triple to drive home a point. In his inaugural promise to the peoples of the Third World, for example, he pledged American help "...not because the communists may be doing it, not because we seek their votes, but because it is right."

But when using doubles and triples to establish cadence, speechwriters should take care that they establish the right order of the elements. Put the big idea at the end. Patrick Henry did not say "Give me death or give me liberty"; Thomas Jefferson did not write: "...[W]e mutually pledge to each other our lives, our sacred honor, and our fortunes."

Sometimes a fourth, fifth, or even more elements can be added to a triple to extend the cadence, change the pace, and offer the speaker a chance to drive home a point. Winston Churchill did this most dramatically in his famous speech to the people of Great Britain following Dunkirk. Notice how, in this passage, the word "fight" marks the cadence and carries a sequence that for many speakers might be too long:

> We shall go on to the end, we shall fight in France, we shall fight on the seas and oceans, we shall fight with growing confidence and strength in the air, we shall defend our island, whatever the cost may be, we shall fight on the beaches, we shall fight in the fields and in the streets, we shall fight in the hills; we shall never surrender....

Recite!

Writers interested in adding the power of cadence to their repertoires would do well to recite aloud the speeches of Lincoln, Churchill, and Franklin Roosevelt, as well as those of the speakers quoted before. Properly phrased, their powerful sentences have the ability to sweep the reader and all else before them. The remarks of these leaders are truly excellent examples of the art of the speechwriter. Two superb resources for developing a feel for cadence are the *Psalms* and the *Book of Common Prayer*, which contain some of the most satisfying rhythms in the English language.

Mastering the art of cadence will not transform your speaker into another Churchill or King; that takes natural gifts on the platform as well as effective prose. But establishing the right rhythms can help your speaker to measure out the stream of words so that those who hear will not only attend the message but will also know they could not have said it better themselves. And that is the first step toward eloquence.

Two "Zen and..." Books

little book called *Zen and the Art of Writing,* by Manjushri Joseph Vitale (Newport Beach, CA: Westcliff Publications, 1984), showed up in the mailbox recently. It is a late addition to the list of "Zen and..." books, a genre of pale imitations spawned by the stunning publishing success of Robert M. Pirsig's *Zen and the Art of Motorcycle Maintenance* (New York: William Morrow, 1974). If you want to write, Vitale avers, all you need do is stand aside and allow what is within to gush forth; "when the muse takes over, you are no longer there. The writing itself is there."

Vitale's premise is that of the entire "Zen and..." movement. Remove the roadblocks to your inner being, master some techniques (meditation, imagery, silence, self-affirmation, etc.), and you can become a great writer, acquire a flawless backhand, or beat the stock market. The trouble is that the same disturbing absence of discipline in Vitale's thinking is, in my view, reflected in his writing. Wishy-washy thought begets pabulum prose.

But I owe a debt to Vitale nonetheless because the main impact of his book was to prompt me to reread Pirsig's masterpiece, which contains some of the best available insight into learning how to write.

Nothing to Say

In one part of the book, Pirsig recounts his professionally difficult experience as a teacher of "freshman comp" in Bozeman, Montana. He'd been having trouble with students who felt they had "nothing to say." One student wanted to write a 500-word essay on "the United States." Pirsig suggested she narrow her topic to just Bozeman. At deadline time, she reported, despondently, that she couldn't think of anything to write. He eventually persuaded her to narrow her scope to the main street of Bozeman, then to part of a single building—the facade of the Opera House—beginning with the top left brick. He got 5,000 words.

The trouble Pirsig diagnosed was that the student had been trying to repeat things she had already heard; her problem was that she was unable to recall anything worth repeating. From this experiment, Pirsig moved on to have his students spend an entire hour writing about the backs of their thumbs, a coin, and other mundane objects. His seminal discovery was one that most writers make the hard way, if they make it at all: There is a profound connection between being able to *see* and being able to write. He says of his students: "For every fact there is an infinity of hypotheses.... Once they got into the idea of seeing directly for themselves, they also saw there was no limit to the amount they could say."

Rules

Another of Pirsig's discoveries about how to write grew out of his attempts to get students to imitate the essays and short stories in their rhetoric and literature texts. The students were seldom successful, in part because the rules they had learned about what made writing work were so full of exceptions, contradictions, and qualifications that an orderly progression from rule to written work became impossible. In fact, it seemed that the rules were "pasted on to the writing after the writing was all done.... It had a certain syrup, as Gertrude Stein once said, but it didn't pour."

The ability to *see* and the daring to suspend the rules (temporarily, at least) when you write are as essential to a writer as reading defenses and "scrambling" are to a quarterback. But there is, of course, a great deal more. Sooner or later both writer and quarterback must submit themselves to the disciplines imposed by the language and the game, because the point of both writing and quarterbacking is to find and take a direction. Contrary to the impression Vitale gives, the internal gusher of creativity is not all there is to writing. It is never mere production but saying something that is as well said as it is worth saying. In other words, the issue is *quality*. And that is why Pirsig's book, for all its agonizing about what quality is, is still worth a writer's time and books like Vitale's, for all their promises about how to achieve quality, are not.

Computers Can't Do It All

*ser friendly* is a bit of computer-age jargon that means the hardware and software of a computer or word processor have simple instructions and are easy for the technologically illiterate to use. Many writers and editors are unable to overcome their Gutenbergianism, however, and harbor the secret suspicion that *user friendly* is actually an ironic expression that borders on self-contradiction, on the order of *airline food* and *part-time parent*. Thoughtful people worry that the computer's user-friendliness threatens to replace the need for essential competence in written communication.

Not to worry, says Sandra E. O'Connell, a consultant specializing in the impact of computer technology on the quality of communication. Speaking in Washington, DC, at an April (1986) meeting of the American Business Communicators, an organization of teachers of business writing, O'Connell reminded her audience that a thorough grounding in the basics of grammar is still essential for coherent expression of thought, "even though your spelling checker works perfectly." Writers who don't bother to learn the difference between *eager* and *anxious* are not going to get much help from computerized thesauruses which don't get into meanings.

"Both the beauty and the utility of language are embedded in its subtlety and complexity," O'Connell said. "Knowing how to make the most of those characteristics will always matter for clear expression."

To function effectively in a user-friendly workplace, O'Connell said, writers and editors also need the following competencies:

♦ Know how to use not only word-processing software but also the thought organizers and programs that assist in the writing task, such as sentence analyzers.

♦ Know how to write simple programs to adapt software to specific tasks. More and more software is being produced with languages that provide flexibility in their use.

♦ Understand your audience and its needs. According to O'Connell, "This is a vastly underrated competency that no computer can ever teach. Real communication requires insight into people's starting points and perspectives."

♦ Be able to analyze, distill, and determine the relevance of the written word. "The ease with which computers can generate words and numbers is seductive," she said. "But they are no substitutes for real knowledge, far less for wisdom. Our user-friendly world needs people who can think. A hoe does not a gardener make; a word processor does not a writer make."

Why Writing Software Is Bad for Good Writers

In a related story appearing in the *Wall Street Journal* (July 7, 1986), David Wessel has argued that writing software (programs devoted to correcting errors in grammar, unclear writing, and poor style) may be able to make bad writing better but may also make good writing worse.

The problem, he has pointed out, is that software is simple-minded. When the computer discovers something it has been programmed not to like, such as a sentence fragment or a passive verb, the writer is told to correct the "error." Nor are style programs very effective. Wessel cited a study done by *PC Magazine*, which estimated that such programs catch only 25 percent of the mistakes that a good human editor would find. Nevertheless, Wessel found several writers who reported that style programs are somewhat useful. Said one: "After it jumps on you about the passive verbs for about the hundredth time, you start trying to avoid them." But such programs are by no means perfect, even in such simple tasks as differentiating from *affect* and *effect*. Grammatik II, for example, doesn't like the perfectly legitimate sentence, "He has a flat affect."

The overall impact of such programs appears to be the flattening of style itself. Wessel subjected his own article to the scrutiny of three different writing programs and, despite his low scores, decided to publish it anyway. We trust some *WSJ* editor was able to improve on Wessel's article and for all our sakes better than any software could have.

Rituals

'm writing this on the bus. Yesterday I found myself scribbling an op ed piece while inbound on the Washington, DC, subway. Last week I was drafting a speech aboard a plane making for Cincinnati. Writing used to be work that had a predictable degree of pace and place associated with the product, but these days it feels as if most of my work is getting done on the way to somewhere else.

The trouble is not just that the pace is frenetic and the tray-tables are a poor substitute for a desk. Nor is it just that the places I'm having to write in are mildly disorienting. It's that the circumstances of my life are forcing me to write beyond the context of ritual, and I don't much like it.

I've always preferred to think that Omar Khayyam extolled the virtues of "a book of verses 'neath the bough" because he was accustomed to writing his verse in such a place; I'm sure the *Rubaiyat* is a creation of this habit. Kant composed his philosophy while staring out his study window at a church steeple; he even had the town fathers of Königsberg lop off a couple of trees when they blocked his view and interfered with his wool-gathering. Thomas Wolfe wrote his novels standing up; he was so tall that he used the top of his refrigerator as a writing desk and finally got to the point where he could scarcely write anywhere else. I understand all that because I can't really write anything I like unless it's quiet, there's a deadline, the books I might need are around, and there's coffee available.

Industrious types pooh-pooh the desk clearing, pencil sharpening, and paper straightening that many of my tribe go through. "Mere delaying tactics," they scoff, "a substitute for the raw courage needed to look the blank page in the eye and begin filling it." There is truth in their scorn, but not the whole truth. Writers know something more: Writing requires rituals.

The specifics of a writer's rituals are, in and of themselves, a matter of indifference. Schiller, after all, needed the smell of rotting apples as his olfactory muse. What does matter is that the writer, like the communicant who goes to the rail, uses a series of patterned acts to construct, brick by brick, a bridge to the point of departure. For the communicant, that departure is into a transcendent realm. Similarly for the writer, rituals serve as stepping-stones to Another Place. The ritualistic acts give rise to words, which, in turn, create something new.

Rituals are also a kind of buffer, an intermediate zone between the quotidian and the slightly altered state of perception that surrounds real writing. For me—and, I think, for most people who write for a living—writing means seeing and thinking about things at more than one level at the same time. A close analogue to this process is what happens when a barbershop quartet warms up: First one singer sounds a note, then each succeeding note is sung in harmony until four different notes have been blended and the song begins. Between the singers and their song is the ritual, the buffer zone they pass through between the ordinariness of singular sound and the slightly altered state of music. They must pass through that zone before they can enter the musical territory they have come to explore and enjoy.

When there isn't time or place for the ritual, the effort often comes out wrong; the words aren't *the* words, or the cadence is off, or the links between the sentences are forged of tissue paper. It's like that on buses, and planes, and the subway. But not where you can make it quiet, when the deadline is palpable, where the books are in reach, and the coffee's still warm.

III.
The Editor's Notebook

Depth at Every Position

ditors are like coaches. The lives of both are dominated by next week's game, and both continually fiddle with "the lineup" in search of the elusive combination of elements that will produce a winner. Coaches characteristically seek the answer to this problem in "depth at every position." They know that without a strong bench, the team can't play well consistently.

The editor's bench is the bookshelf. Here, too, the name of the game is depth at every position. Editors need two or three general dictionaries, each with its singular advantages. To these should be added dictionaries peculiar to the special areas of publishing in which they are engaged, e.g., medicine, engineering, computers. Editors in specialized areas should also consider adding one or more of the *Oxford Companion to...* volumes to their working libraries. These works cover such topics as theater, music, English literature, the mind, and American literature. There should be several books on writing, style, usage, and grammar. Perhaps there will be a book on lexicography or the history of English. There definitely ought to be one or two collections of quotations, a good typography manual, as well as works on editing and proofreading.

Like the coach's bench, this bookshelf is where the editor goes to meet critical situations. But editors will always have some area where they feel slightly insecure. Here are some suggestions for backup strength in the areas where you, gentle reader, may feel weak.

Dictionaries

For the desk, the standard is fast becoming *Webster's New World Dictionary of the American Language* (New York: Warner Books, 1982). It is the recommended desk dictionary at *The New York Times*, Associated Press, and United Press International. For the second team, choose either the *American Heritage Dictionary* (Boston: Houghton-Mifflin, 1982) or the *Oxford American Dictionary* (New

York: Oxford University Press, 1980) for their usage notes. But for the pure at heart, *Webster's Second International* (out of print) remains the apotheosis of lexicography; many *New World* users specify it for backup. *Webster III* (1961) aroused a hornet's nest among purists when it came out for being "too permissive." The two-volume, compact edition of the *Oxford English Dictionary* (New York: Oxford University Press, 1986) remains, of course, the best possible reason for joining the Book-of-the-Month Club (although you don't get the supplements). For recent additions to the language, the *Random House Dictionary of the English Language* (New York: Random House, second unabridged edition, 1987) is best.

Usage

Here, happily, the depth problem can be solved readily. Most editors know and use several standard works, but Roy Copperud's *American Usage and Style: The Consensus* (New York: Van Nostrand Reinhold, 1979) achieves depth in a single volume by comparing books by nine major usage authorities (Theodore Bernstein, Margaret M. Bryant, Roy Copperud, Cornelia and Bergen Evans, Rudolf Flesch, Wilson Follett, H.W. Fowler/Sir Ernest Gowers, Nathan and Sylvia Mager, and William and Mary Morris) and summarizing their views. It is the most helpful book in print on usage. For runner-up, I would nominate *Success With Words* (Pleasantville, NY: Reader's Digest, 1983).

Style

The equivalent to Copperud in the area of style is *Words Into Type* (Englewood Cliffs, NJ: Prentice-Hall, 1974) by Marjorie Skillin and Robert Gay. In addition to their comprehensive treatment of style, Skillin and Gay provide a large grammar section, as well as chapters on such topics as preparing manuscripts for publication, copyright, reading copy, typography, and commonly confused words. They also include a thorough discussion of printing technology and an exhaustive glossary of printing and typesetting terms.

Grammar

Many editors will have a copy of George Kittredge and Frank Farley's *Advanced English Grammar* (New York: AMS Press., Inc., Reprint of 1913) or for quick reference a student handbook like the *Harbrace College Handbook* (San Diego: Harcourt Brace Jovanovich, 1984) by John C. Hodges and Mary E. Whitten. But for real depth you can't beat George O. Curme's *A Grammar of the English Language*

(Old Lyme, CT: Verbatim Books, 1983). Finding one's way around the two volumes (*Parts of Speech* and *Syntax*) takes getting used to, as does Curme's occasionally recondite style (here the depth threatens to become bottomless), but if you are looking for a discussion of the optative subjunctive, you will find it here. Examples are superabundant.

Thesaurus

Here I would favor putting Roget on the bench and putting another, less well known work in the starting lineup. The best English thesaurus in print is *The Synonym Finder* by J.I. Rodale, as completely revised by Laurence Urdang (Emmaus, PA: Rodale Press, 1978). It contains more than a million synonyms arranged alphabetically; thus, you don't have to look up everything twice, as when using Roget.

Book of Quotations

The main entry sections of the standard works are arranged chronologically (*Bartlett's Familiar Quotations*) and alphabetically by author (*The Oxford Dictionary of Quotations*). Either is fine for checking quotations, but topically arranged volumes are more useful when looking for an apt line to spice up a piece of writing. Here again, depth comes from two seldom-mentioned works. *Webster's Treasury of Relevant Quotations* (Springfield, MA: Merriam-Webster, 1978, out of print) by Edward F. Murphy provides access to many quotable writers who do not appear in other collections. The *Dictionary of Quotations* (New York: Delacorte, 1968, out of print), edited by Bergen Evans, arranges quotations chronologically within topics. The book also provides many subcategories—under "Love," for example, there are 26; under "God," 9.

History of English

As critic John Simon has written, "Was there ever a more stirring, more enduring epic than the story of the English tongue?" Two relatively recent works stand out in this area—Robert Claiborne's *Our Marvelous Native Tongue* (New York: Times Books, 1983) and *The Story of English* by Robert McCrum, William Cran, and Robert MacNeil (New York: Viking, 1986), which served as the complement to the wonderful PBS series on the subject. The former work is somewhat more scholarly, although still eminently readable, the latter less a work in linguistic history than in sociolinguistics, and on that account vastly more entertaining. Either or both belong on the bookshelf of the editor seeking to round out his or her library.

Lexicography

Resources about dictionary making do not readily come to the attention of the nonspecialist, a category that includes most editors. A single volume will suffice, and for those truly interested it should be comprehensive enough to provide historical background in lexicography, an orientation to the key elements of a good dictionary (e.g., etymology, pronunciation, synonymy, the front matter, definition making, usage, and other basics). Fortunately, Sidney I. Landau's *The Art and Craft of Lexicography* (New York: Charles Scribner's Sons, 1984) fills the bill on all counts. Especially useful is the annotated bibliography of 51 dictionaries, included as an appendix.

General Knowledge and Fact Checking

As is well known, *The Encyclopedia Britannica* (Chicago: Encyclopedia Britannica Ed., 1987) is not a handy desk reference. The *New Columbia Encyclopedia* (New York: Columbia University Press, 1975) is an excellent one-volume reference book—in my view the best. To acquire depth, however, editors should have a copy of *The Harper Dictionary of Modern Thought* (out of print), edited by Alan Bullock and Oliver Stallybrass, which contains thumbnail descriptions of many topics Columbia doesn't deal with, such as *multivariate analysis, fiscal policy,* and *social Darwinism.* For checking facts, it's still hard to beat *The World Almanac and Book of Facts* (New York: Newspaper Enterprise Assn.), or the *Information Please Almanac* (Boston: Houghton-Mifflin), both published annually. Many editors simply buy them in alternate years. Where else can you find out that the name for a group of foxes is a *skulk* and that three denominations of U.S. currency do not carry pictures of presidents ($10, Hamilton; $100, Franklin; $10,000, Chase). That, fellow coaches, is depth.

"...The Innocent, the Eager, and the Doomed"

he title is borrowed. It is the tail end of the sub-title Karen Elizabeth Gordon has given to two uproariously instructive books: *The Well-Tempered Sentence: A Punctuation Handbook for...* (New York: Ticknor & Fields, 1983) and *The Transitive Vampire: A Handbook of Grammar for...* (New York: Times Books, 1984). If you have ever harbored the heresy that grammar and punctuation, however necessary to clear thought and expression, are irretrievably dull, these little books will restore your faith in orthodoxy.

Punctuation

The Well-Tempered Sentence is nothing more than a presentation of the rules governing the standard marks of punctuation, a chapter per mark, with examples. But that is like saying the Louvre is a presentation of the rules governing composition, light, line, and color, with examples. It is Gordon's examples that beguile. They are weird, whimsical, antic. Her theory seems to be that seduction is superior to blatant pedagogy and a lot more fun. That is as good an approach to learning punctuation and grammar as any; it is better than most. Some rules and examples follow:

Rule: "Two or more verbs having the same subject are not to be separated by commas."

Example: "Rosamund counted her lymph nodes and then returned to the tabulation of her toes."

Rule: "Three or more elements in a series are separated by commas."

Example: "Across her pellucid and guileless complexion danced a motley choir of alibis, innuendoes, disguises, and sobriquets."

Rule: "The semicolon goes outside quotation marks or parentheses."

Example: "Not only were we naked, crazed, and starved (and far from our warm little homes); we were without any good books as well."

Grammar

Gordon comes right out and admits that she is playing a dangerous game in *The Transitive Vampire*, "smuggling the injunction of grammar into your cognizance through a ménage of revolving lunatics kidnapped into this book." Ménage, indeed. *Vampire* is populated with all manner of dragons, gargoyles, angels, wolves, nymphs, and indifferently draped voluptuaries, carried off from books of the sort that give *kitsch* a bad name. But, she says comfortingly, "if you nuzzle these pages with abandon, writing will lose its terror and your sentences their disarray."

On verbs, Gordon insists that "the verb is the heartthrob of the sentence," whether transitive ("We bounced the idea around the saloon") or intransitive ("Nemo slouched past the fountain"). Verbals, on the other hand, such as infinitives and gerunds, are not verbs because they don't assert anything; instead, they are used as other parts of speech. An infinitive can be a noun ("Sylvie loves to split infinitives") or an adverb ("Osbert was difficult to lose"). A gerund, always a noun, can thus be a direct object ("He craves flogging") or the object of a preposition ("By dunking her crumpet in the marmalade, Melissa committed a midafternoon *faux pas*").

Tackling one of the favorite topics of a long-time speechwriter, she insists that "rhythm is as important a part of a well-written sentence as grammatical correctness." Notice how short and simple sentences can be changed....

"Yolanda became tipsy. She felt a rage for life. It was surging. An attractive new trauma caused this. She was yanked out of her tedium" becomes "Yanked out of her tedium by an attractive new trauma, Yolanda became tipsy with a surging rage for life."

For all the fun Gordon provides, there is also a practical point to all this. Editors who supervise writers might adopt the subtlety of acquiring these books and strewing them on a convenient end table. They can be used to settle a lot of arguments about comma splices and when to use a colon, but any standard work can do that. What no standard work can do is get people talking about language. Yolanda and her clique will do the trick.

Developing a Writer's Voice

ducation writer Joseph Featherstone once characterized the writing of John Dewey as having "the monotonous consistency of peanut butter." Whether or not they agree about Dewey's writing, most editors agree that writers who work hard at it develop styles of their own (creative writing teachers call it "finding your own voice"). Sometimes style achieves the level of self-portraiture, to the point that the writer cannot be mistaken for anyone else: Joyce and Hemingway are good examples. Obviously, this does not happen often, but when it does, writer and editor are entitled to apply for a joint appointment to *The New Yorker*.

Many editors can nevertheless help the writers they supervise to develop their own styles. By attending to a few simple precepts, editors can guide new writers in the right direction.

Presumption

The first lesson the editor must teach is that style is not simply "the dress of thoughts." Lord Chesterfield was wrong when he defined style this way, because his idea presumes that language and thought can somehow be separated. They cannot. The purpose of style is not to take an idea and dress it up, but to put an idea before the reader in the form that comes naturally to the writer and goes just as naturally to the mind of the reader. Here, the medium truly becomes the message. An idea is not a department store window to be trimmed but an opening into the world.

It follows that style is not a form of exhibitionism, a parade of long words the writer knows or of verbal pyrotechnics, à la Spiro Agnew's "nattering nabobs of negativism." Style is, in the words of Swift, "proper words in proper places."

A Lesson from Milton

The next task of the editor is to make sure the writer works at mastering the writing craft. I remember reading once about a class on Milton taught by W.H. Auden at the University of Michigan. He required that each of his charges look up every single word of Milton's *Lycidas* in the *Oxford English Dictionary* (228 lines!). The poem begins,

"Yet once more, O ye laurels, and once more,

Ye myrtles brown, with ivy never sere...."

The students discovered that although the entries for words like *laurels* were rather long, the entries of words like *yet* were even longer.

Editors interested in developing new writers should encourage them to take a piece of submitted or assigned work and do Auden's *OED* exercise on some portion of it. This forced immersion in the sea of language can have two effects, both of them healthy. First, rubbing the writer's nose in every word tends to point up the defects of overblown prose. Whatever its other effects, the tedium produced by such an exercise certainly gives a new writer a generous regard for economy of expression. Second, and far more important, time spent perusing the dictionary creates a new respect for the power of mundane words, such as Milton's *once, more, and, with,* and *never.* Familiar words are the workhorses of good writing, and the more deeply writers understand them, the better their writing will be.

Analysis, Writing, Rewriting

Editors should also encourage new writers to become thoroughly familiar with their own writing. Here are some questions writers should ask themselves:

♦ What kinds of sentences do I write (compound, complex, compound-complex)? What kinds do I avoid?

♦ What is the ratio of transitive to intransitive verbs in my writing? Active to passive constructions? Adjectives to nouns? Adverbs to verbs?

♦ How orthodox are my grammar and syntax? Are my reasons for breaking rules good (they serve the piece) or not so good (showing off)?

♦ Am I partial to particular figures of speech (metaphors, similes) or constructions (not only...but also; either...or; both...and; on the one hand...on the other hand)?

♦ How many of the expressions in my writing are really clichés?

Editors prospecting for and nurturing writing talent should also instruct new writers in the art of writing with cadence. (Technical writing is an exception.) A style without cadence is a parade without a drummer; let it go on for long and its feet get tangled. Speechwriting is a particularly good training ground for developing this most neglected stylistic tool. A particularly fine lesson in cadences is provided on pp. 107-108 of James J. Kilpatrick's *The Writer's Art* (Kansas City, MO: Andrews, McMeel & Parker, Inc., 1984), where Kilpatrick walks readers through the construction of one of his columns.

But one of the best ways for new writers to acquire a style, better than analyzing their own prose, is to produce it. Writing forces the writer to make choices, and exercising the muscles of selection and rejection turns a novice into a real writer. (Editors have a self-interest in these gymnastics because the more ruthlessly writers edit their own writing, the easier the editor's job.)

Even better than writing, of course, is rewriting and, in this vein, a thoughtful gift for a promising writer is a framed motto from Dr. Johnson: "Read over your composition, and when you meet with a passage that you think particularly fine, strike it out."

Turabian's Classic Reaches the Half-Century Mark

ust about everyone who ever went to college—and quite a few high school grads as well—knows the name of Kate L. Turabian. Her *Manual for Writers of Term Papers, Theses, and Dissertations* (Chicago: University of Chicago Press, 1973) has sold more than 5.3 million copies in its various editions. No wonder. It is the one book that helped many of us fight eight bouts of end-of-semester panic.

The most wonderful thing about that book was that there was no way it could be stumped: If you wanted to know when to use an ellipsis and when not, and what kind to use, Turabian had the answer. If you didn't know how to organize your data into a table or a chart—or worse, didn't know which was appropriate—you looked it up in Turabian. Never mind that you didn't know how to footnote a taped interview with someone you traveled 100 miles to talk to for your senior thesis; Turabian did. After 50 years, her work is that rarest of publishing rarities, a reference book best seller. And it deserves to be one.

Never a group to miss a trick, the University of Chicago Press brought out (May 29, 1987) a 5th edition of her classic to celebrate its 50th year in print. It is now 300 pages long (completely revised and enlarged), has a 17-page index, and the cost is still well within the reach of the average student.

Turabian was an unlikely candidate to become the Miss Manners of the Academy. The little pamphlet that grew to become the near-universal arbiter of academic style was basically an act of self-defense. Hired by the University of Chicago in 1925 as a departmental secretary, she moved to the Press to become Dissertation Secretary. That meant having to examine theses and dissertations for form. Then, as now, too many students were poor spellers, punctuators, and stylists. She saw the need for a brief reference work that would do for typewritten research papers what the University's *Manual of Style* did for typeset work.

At first, Turabian distributed her pamphlet to doctoral candidates for free. But once the word got out, the university bookstore began selling it, finally copyrighting it in 1937. The first advertising was nothing more than a two-line ad in *Publishers Weekly*. By 1949, the pamphlet had grown to a 68-page paperback with annual sales in excess of 20,000 copies.

Turabian remained active in preparing the succeeding editions (1955, 1967, 1973) of her "little book," revisions intended to bring the book into conformity with the Press's *Manual of Style* and with changing trends in academic writing. The 5th edition, revised by Bonnie Honigsblum, was sparked by the preparation of the 13th edition of the Chicago *Manual of Style* and the changes brought on by computerized word processing. A survey of several hundred deans and dissertation secretaries provided data for revisions.

Although the "intellectual heroine of the Middle West" (which was what we history majors at my undergraduate institution called her) retired in 1958, Turabian's *Manual for Writers* remains the definitive "how to" book for passing Western Civ and Principles of _____(fill in the blank). Indeed, for academic writing, it is the original self-publishing manual. The new edition has completely revised guidelines for preparing manuscripts and, appropriately, focuses on the needs of computer users. (The index entry under "Computerized word processing" runs to two full columns, exceeded only by that for "Notes.")

Now in her nineties, Turabian has always been amazed by the recognition her "little book" has brought her. She shouldn't be. Like all good pieces of written work, it endures because it was based on a simple idea, well organized in pursuit of its aims, and, above all, useful.

Author's Note: Kate Turabian died late in 1987.

*On Pilgrimage**

he goal of the Muslim's pilgrimage is the Kaaba in Mecca; for the Jew it is the Wailing Wall in Jerusalem; for the Roman Catholic, St. Peter's in Rome. Last July, I made a pilgrimage to London to pay homage and receive inspiration. Although no religious sentiment was involved, a faith of a different kind was renewed.

The destination was Number 17, Gough Square, just behind Fleet Street, a four-story townhouse indistinguishable from scores of others all over London. Yet it is visited by thousands of pilgrims annually. Why? Because here is where Dr. Johnson compiled his monumental *A Dictionary of the English Language* (1755).

As with most places of pilgrimage, it is not the place itself that makes the visit worthwhile, but what happened there. Johnson rented the house in 1746, using part of the proceeds from a contract with a consortium of publishing sponsors. The four-story house was large and handsome for its time, providing living quarters for Johnson and his wife and, in the spacious garret, space for dictionary making. Within this space of perhaps 15' x 35' Johnson achieved what his biographer, W. Jackson Bate, has characterized as "one of the greatest single achievements of scholarship, perhaps the greatest ever performed by one individual...in a comparable length of time." (It took Johnson 9 years to make his dictionary; 40 members of l'Academie Française took 55 years to compile a definitive dictionary of French.)

Although the garret is now almost empty, it is easy to imagine the disarray inevitably associated with so great a work, the piles and piles of books from which Johnson's assistants copied out the quotations he had marked to illustrate how words were used. Boswell described the garret as "fitted up like a countinghouse," with a long desk running the length of the room where clerks could work while standing. With Bate, one can well envisage the corpulent figure of

---

*Author's Note: Historical details for this piece were gleaned from *Samuel Johnson,* by W. Jackson Bate, (New York: Harcourt Brace Jovanovitch, 1977).

the Doctor himself, perched precariously atop his three-legged elbowchair, which had to be jammed against one wall to keep it—and him—from falling over.

But it is the work itself that inspires the pilgrim's awe. It is easy to forget, in these times when each new dictionary is laid brick-like atop those troweled in before it, how mind-bendingly difficult Johnson's labors must have been. (His dictionary was not, as is often thought, the first. There were a few predecessors; although some had merit, most were little more than lists of "hard words.") In his garret, Johnson composed the definitions—and illumined the shades of meaning—for more than 40,000 words, illustrating their diverse senses with more than 114,000 quotations drawn from every field of learning since the middle of the Elizabethan period. In the end, he used only about half the quotations he had collected.

Concept and Method

What distinguished Johnson's work was its conceptual originality. His lexicographical laboratory consisted of about 80 large notebooks. For each word, he did not begin a definition for which he then sought to glean the supporting illustrations. Instead he started with the best usage, from which he then worked to penetrate to the heart of meaning. He carefully read the works of as many writers as he could whose use of English he admired, marking the sentences he wanted to quote and noting in the margins the word under which he wanted each quotation to appear. These books he would deliver to clerks, who transcribed the quotes on individual slips of paper, arranging them chronologically under the word referred to in order to give some sense of each word's historical development. Nuances of meaning were sorted out, and when each word was thus circumscribed by the way or ways it was used, its definition was written. Only then did Johnson consult other dictionaries, not for corrections but to see if he had forgotten anything.

Where Johnson's work has excelled all others—before or since—is in these definitions. So successful were they that Noah Webster's *American Dictionary of the English Language* (1828) was still highly derivative of Johnson's. The usage notations served Johnson well, as with a verb like *fall*, for which he managed to find illustrations for some 64 distinguishable meanings. Many of Johnson's definitions are still cited as examples of his wit: for example, "*oats*—a grain, which in England is generally given to horses, but in Scotland supports the people"; "*lexicographer*—a writer of dictionaries; a harmless drudge"; "*patron*—commonly a wretch who supports with insolence and is paid with flattery."

When finally published in two volumes, the dictionary made Johnson not merely famous but renowned throughout Europe; George III offered him a pension, which afforded enough economic security to enable him to devote most of his time to writing.

For many, Dr. Johnson remains impossibly remote—fit company only for historians, or a textbook creature like Addison or Steele. But for those who love English, the sound and the sense of it, he is never far off. If you make a pilgrimage to 17, Gough Square, if you climb to the garret and listen closely, you can still hear Johnson's tread on the stair, still see him in the corner, writing. Two centuries later, there is comfort in the sound and sight of him.

The Good, the Bad, and the Fuzzy

arry Speakes, Ronald Reagan's former "spokesman" has—by his own admission—made up quotations and put them in the president's mouth. On one occasion, Speakes, apparently upset that the president was being upstaged during the 1987 Washington summit, "quoted" a private remark Reagan never made to Gorbachev. On another, Speakes admits to having taken some remarks by Secretary of State George Schultz in a Cabinet meeting and put them on the president's lips.

Aside from the implications and risks (and they are by no means minimal) assumed by the nation when underlings go around telling the world that the president of the United States has said things that he has not, Speakes's revelation raises concerns of intrinsic interest to editors. The discussion about Speakes's admission casts light on three different kinds of quotations: those that are well within the limits, the definite no-nos, and fuzzy "borderline" quotations.

The Good

Everyone agrees that the best kind of quotation is something the person actually said, reported accurately, warts and all. No problem there, and no need for a "spin doctor," that is, a highly paid PR expert who advises on how the thing will play in Boise and who uses the thesaurus accordingly.

Less pure are "accurate" quotations that have been slightly altered prior to publication, "altered" in this case meaning some oral padding has been left out for conciseness or nonsubstantive grammatical errors have been eliminated. Examples:

Verbal padding

In the verbatim statement, "Profits for the last three months—[January, February, and March]—have not been as high as for the three months previous [that is, for October, November, and December,]," the bracketed material might well be deleted by a space-conscious editor. No substantive change would occur; the post- and predeletion senses are the same. The punctilious would add appropriate ellipses.

Corrected grammar

In the verbatim quotation, "Everyone involved got what was coming to [them]," the conscientious editor could change the bracketed word to *him* (if gender is not an issue) without losing his or her license or becoming a moral leper. Again, no substantive issue is involved; the speaker, the language, and the truth—if not the absolute truth—are all served.

This sort of change is made all the time and no one thinks much about it, although rethinking it from time to time to reestablish limits firmly in an editor's mind is not a bad idea. The editor does not draw breath who does not think (and usually correctly) that he or she could clarify a speaker's thought by "cleaning up" a quotation. When that slippery slope beckons, however, editors need to remember that the ride can end in disaster.

The Bad

At the other end of the spectrum is a cynical kind of quote manufacturing and tampering that plays fast and loose with the truth and has consequences reaching far beyond the mechanics of attribution. The Speakes defense, that after many years he "understood the mind of the president" well enough to be able to represent him between quotation marks without Reagan's knowledge, comes perilously close to a kind of god-playing.

Writers whose jobs require them to help others represent themselves to the public (e.g., speechwriters, press secretaries, and corporate communications officers who are *paid* to understand the boss's mind and come up with the words that will advance the boss's goals) have to fight continually the temptation to which Speakes succumbed. And, when it comes to deciding what words of the boss will get into print, editors of company publications are often caught in an ethical crossfire—between the canons of personal and editorial ethics, the legitimate demands of the job, and the not unnatural desire to cooperate in putting the best public face on one's employer.

But there are some clear limits. Company officials, reports, and newsletters should not manufacture quotations that lie to the stockholders, for example. Writers and editors should not allow themselves to become party to public information efforts that could harm people. And company editors should protest efforts, however well intentioned, to turn the publications shop into an organizational ministry of propaganda.

Indeed, there is virtue in telling the truth about oneself even when the truth is not flattering, especially when a goodly portion of the audience knows the truth anyway. Ignoring or refusing to admit the truth only makes the speaker—whether an individual or a multinational corporation—look silly. Contrary to the prevailing wisdom, good quotesmanship is *not* cleverly concealed prevarication; it is helping the speaker find the words that *honorably* express the speaker's intent.

The Fuzzy

This brings us to the realm of "manufactured quotes," a genre that every editor and journalist knows well. The most innocent example goes something like this. A long-time, valued employee retires. The PR department grinds out a press release. In the release, President Brown of Apex Industries announces the retirement to the trade press, embellished with a manufactured remark that goes something like this: "We are truly sorry to see Charlie Johnson leave us. Our company and, indeed, our entire industry will miss him."

Editors who receive such releases are well aware that Brown probably never said anything of the sort and, assuming they will do a story based on the release, will do one of three things about it: (1) delete the quotation, (2) have a reporter call Brown to get something more substantial, or (3) take the path of least resistance and print the quotation, secure in the knowledge that, had he been asked, Brown would have said something very like what was in the press release, all the while trusting that the public record can survive such an assault on the truth, which it indeed can. Nevertheless, in taking option (3) the editor does commit an untruth and a disservice to his own readers, albeit one somewhat on the order of volubly admiring Aunt Agnes's new hat. For the most part, the "No harm-No foul" rule applies.

But the untruths and disservices committed by junior-league Larry Speakeses, although widely viewed as part of the game, can readily take on an insidious quality when more is at stake than saying the "right" or "expected" thing. Sooner or later, the line is crossed between what was really said and what people—even the people in charge—wish *had* been said. Even worse, what tends to happen is that made-up quotations come to be regarded by an audience as the truth because they say relatively predictable things.

Image replaces reality; the press release or newsletter article becomes a verbal Potëmkin village.

The most important issue of principle here is not whether the quoted person actually said the quoted words. The real problem lies in the distorted relationship this practice creates among the quoter, the quoted, and the audience. All are now forced to play false: (1) the quoter, who, because the reality created by the quotation must be defended, has to lie even further; (2) the quoted, who, because the words have been published with his or her name behind them, must either believe them or become duplicitous, and (3) the members of the audience, who, because their trust is repeatedly betrayed, eventually become cynical out of self-protection. In other words, the real problem is what happens to the human spirit. We lose each other.

One constructive way of dealing with the problem is for editors to take the initiative. All of us should work to become aware of those occasions when a quotable statement may be called for. If the statement is actually drafted or dictated, the editor can then edit—for approval. If the boss asks to have something drafted, the editor becomes a ghostwriter and will have to work out a different set of ethical considerations. In either case, the editor can become part of a process of creating the truth instead of manipulating it.

IV.
Usage

Modifier Madness

he ability of one part of speech to fill the shoes of another is one of the most delightful features of English. Using adjectives as nouns ("seeing red") or verbs as adjectives ("open door") makes for much creativity and flexibility. Among the most common crossovers is the use of nouns as adjectives. In English any noun can be used this way (at least theoretically), and there is no end to the useful—and quite appropriate—constructions that can be cobbled together by pressing nouns into service as modifiers: *house party, love story, Bronze Age, postage stamp.*

But things have gotten out of hand. Modifier madness is starting to overload the conceptual circuitry. Most of us can still handle tripartite phrases like *test ban treaty, silicone floor wax,* or *aluminum rocket booster;* these are small potatoes. By the time we move on to constructions like *Steamfitters Union Perpetual Insurance Income Fund,* queasiness begins to set in. And a chasm separates these from the advertisement for a recent colloquium offered by the Goddard Space Flight Center: *Erasable Gigabyte Magneto-optic Data Storage Discs.*

Noun Strings from Wall Street

But the gigabyters are still playing in the bush leagues compared to the Wall Streeters. This whopper recently found its way to the top of the in-basket: "By pooling the resources of many investors into a limited partnership, it is possible for individuals to benefit from the multimillion dollar data management peripheral equipment leasing industry."

I count eight modifiers: one article (the); one adjective-adverb combination (multimillion); two "pure" nouns (dollar, data); two nouns derived from verbs (management, equipment); one verbal noun (leasing); and one borderline adjective-noun (peripheral). (In computerese, *peripheral* is a noun, as in "Our CPU supports 24 peripherals.") All these are stacked atop a single noun, whose knees are clearly at the buckle. The construction is a ponderous inverted pyramid, in which all the conceptual weight bears down on a hapless *industry.*

The result is a mountain of conceptual rubble. Does the industry under discussion manage data or lease peripherals? Or does it lease peripherals that manage data? Is it the peripheral equipment that is in the multimillion-dollar range in terms of its value, or the industry as a whole in terms of its revenues? Or is it only important to know that, whatever is going on, big bucks can be made?

The Need for Brevity

So much of this kind of language comes at us from advertising ("New Formula Instant Chicken Noodle Soup Mix!") and the newspaper headlines ("Chemical Waste Disposal Task Force Convenes") that it can't be avoided. The need for brevity jams words and ideas into the closest possible proximity, the better to blitzkrieg the reader. And, like an airborne virus, modifier madness soon infects everyone in the village.

Beyond the ads and the newspapers, modifier madness is nurtured not only by English's enormous flexibility but also because it is endlessly forgiving. A sentence whose nouns are freighted with modifiers can remain impeccably grammatical, even as it mounts its assault on rationality. Words, unlike mathematical symbols, do not always gain elegance from brevity. Stacking nouns and adjectives does achieve brevity, but beyond a certain point, what is gained to brevity is lost to clarity. Our Mother Tongue may be endlessly forgiving, but in the end it's the reader who always pays the price for her sweet disposition.

Redundancy: Empty Calories for the Mind

 riters are like fatties; they have to work at their verbal waistlines every day. The equivalent of junk food for the writer is redundancy, and the job of the editor is to count calories and impose diets. The temptation to gorge on empty calories arises from motives both noble ("I want to give just the right shade of meaning") and base ("The metaphor is so good I can't bear to give it up"). But the temptation must be resisted.

In Many Guises

Redundancy takes several forms. One is tautology, in which the same idea is repeated in different words without adding to sense or rhetorical effect: "The foreman said only one additional worker has been added to the night shift." Another is periphrasis or circumlocution—talking around the subject. A common example is the *not un-* construction, as in "She was not unsympathetic to his overtures." This way of putting things runs the not unreal danger of becoming not unarch after a while.

Another form of redundancy is plain overwriting. Consistently using constructions like *at this point in time* for *now* or *in the immediate vicinity* for *near* is simply overkill.

Another contribution to the linguistic spare tire is the pleonasm. Pleonasms are to ideas what chocolate sauce is to the brownie—too much of a good thing. Several seem to be making the rounds, some predictable and harmless, others more troublesome. Most writers and editors are alert to the fact that *unique* should not be qualified. But English suffers a body blow every time a congressional committee delves into the *true facts*, or the school board reaches a *shared consensus*, or the company adopts a *recent innovation*.

Thinking It Through

Part of the problem, of course, is that people don't think about the full meanings of the words they use. Usage authority Roy

Copperud's *American Usage and Style: The Consensus.* (New York: Van Nostrand Reinhold, 1979) points out, for example, that words like *custom, experience, events, records,* and *history* are basically tied to the past. Using *past* to modify them is pleonastic. Similarly, *plans, prospects,* and *developments* are tied to the future; phrases like *advance planning* and *advance reservations* are one word too long.

When the connotations of a word are ambiguous, context usually supplies clarity. *Records* do not have associations only with the past, as any sports fan will tell you. But when some pole vaulter clears 20 feet the achievement need not be designated a *new* record; the adjective is superfluous.

A Free Gift

So, for what it's worth, here's some advance warning. The ups and downs of the writing life may put a smile on your lips or a frown on your forehead—either can be the end result. But above all, remember to bring these points to mind whenever a manuscript is in close proximity; they have a way of eventuating in outcomes that will remain perpetual for all time. In that case, the best thing you can do is maintain your equanimity of mind and avoid redundancies, again and again.

Oxymorons

urn it inside out and you may be able to find another use for it," my old logic prof used to say. If a pleonasm is a rhetorical figure in which the nominally obvious is adjectivally belabored, as when the *widow woman* goes to the *funeral service* after her husband has run afoul of the *lone gunman*, then turning the idea of the pleonasm inside out gives you the oxymoron.

Ask any ten people to guess what an oxymoron is and eight of them are likely to tell you it's a new detergent. But the word is actually a combination of two Greek words, *oxys* (*sharp*) and *moros* (*dull*). The term is thus itself an oxymoron, a *sharp dullness* in the metaphorical sense of being *clever-foolish*. An oxymoron is something like a neatly tied together contradiction, as when Chaucer calls poverty a *hateful good*, and Yeats refers to "...the murderous innocence of the sea."

The fact that writers of this stature use them to such good effect already differentiates oxymorons from pleonasms, which are almost always excess verbal baggage. Oxymoronic expressions gain force from the seeming absurdity they bring to mind. It is this forcefulness that makes oxymorons among the most effective figures of speech. They work especially well in poetry ("No light, but rather darkness visible."—*Milton*), politics ("the loyal opposition"), and humor ("My wife has a whim of iron."—*Oliver Herford*). Oscar Wilde's masterly oxymoron, "He hasn't a single redeeming vice," shows that oxymorons can be ironic as well as funny.

Handle with Care

But as the great H.W. Fowler warns, "the figure needs discreet handling or its effect may become absurd rather than impressive." Or, he might have added, it may quickly degenerate to the level of cliché, e.g., *sounds of silence, open secret*, and *conspicuously absent.*

One particularly delightful form of oxymoronic thought is found in the *bull*, a self-contradictory proposition, e.g., "If you're going to stand on this corner, you'll have to move along." Yogi Berra was famous for them: "Toots Shor's restaurant is so crowded nobody goes there anymore"; "If nobody wants to come out to the ballpark, nobody's going to stop them."

But the undisputed king of the bull and master of the oxymoron was the late Hollywood producer, Samuel Goldwyn, who was famous for his logic stoppers (both deliberate and innocent), e.g., "A bachelor's life is no life for a single man"; "It's more than magnificent, it's mediocre!" Many Goldwynisms have crept into everyday parlance: "I can give you a definite maybe," "Let's have some new clichés," and "Include me out."

What does all this mean? Well, think of it this way. The next time a conversation turns to airline food, military intelligence, or contemporary rock music, at least you'll know what name to call it.

Weeds

f a weed is a plant growing somewhere you don't want it, then jargon is the weedpatch of language. Thus, I don't hold with H.W. Fowler, who defines jargon as "talk that is considered both ugly sounding and hard to understand." Ugliness is in the eye of the beholder, and while a word like "byte" may be ugly to some, it is elegant to a computer programmer, for whom it expresses a precise and therefore clear meaning. It isn't that jargon is noxious in itself, it's that, like crabgrass, the dratted stuff keeps rooting where it doesn't belong.

Jargon creates two difficulties, both of which endanger clear understanding. The first is seldom mentioned: Jargon deflects the attention of the reader away from the subject at hand and onto the writer. And, truth to tell, this is why most of us lapse into jargon; we succumb to the temptation to parade our command of various and arcane vocabularies. But the business writer who lapses into computerese while discussing the latest movie risks losing the reader's attention and respect. Or, as Dick Cavett puts it, "Anyone who uses the words 'parameter' and 'interface' should never be invited to a dinner party."

The Style of Jargon

The second difficulty is a more common complaint. Jargon, because it is language misdirected, soon becomes soporific and finally narcotic. It depends on a prose style that sooner or later becomes a candidate for the putdown C. Wright Mills once made on the writing of fellow sociologist Talcott Parsons: "Talcott writes with ink of opium on pages of lead." Jargon prefers the noun to the verb; its building blocks are smothered verbs and the prepositional phrase that trail in their wake. Among the most common constructions of jargon-laden writing is the all too familiar: "the (choose any verb)tion of (choose any noun)." Thus, like the builders of the Tower of Babel, the architects of jargon court the confusion of tongues as they stack their nouns one atop another. The jargon-laden style uses bricks without the mortar of thought; in the end, the sentences and paragraphs simply collapse.

On examination, both these problems turn out to have a moral dimension; both are a refusal to apply standards, in the one case to the writer and in the other to the product. Allowing the weeds of jargon to grow all over the garden is basically a refusal to say that this is good writing and that is bad writing. The willingness of writers and editors to make such distinctions and the implicit trust of the reader that the writer will make them are part of the moral bond between them, and jargon threatens the integrity of this bond.

Two Responses

The conventional response to the moral problem of jargon is a kind of moralism, a "tsk-tsking" of the kind that most of us learned from our eighth-grade English teachers. We hear their echoes today in the tough cadences of those Kojaks of the English language, Edwin Newman and John Simon. But the cure of moralism is no cure at all and often is worse than the disease. It changes so little and risks so much goodwill from people who might otherwise be disposed to curb their jargoneering; self-righteousness is a taste only angels can afford to cultivate.

But there is another way. Richard A. Lanham, in his intriguing little book, *Style: An Anti-Textbook* (New Haven: Yale University Press, 1974), suggests that a more fruitful approach is to think of jargon as an effort toward a real style, however clumsy. His point is not that we should indulge ourselves in a kind of linguistic Grundyism, but that we start translating jargon into real English, and thereby get some fun out of all the special little lingoes each of us dabbles in from time to time. His advice is to stop being linguistic police and to start becoming connoisseurs of jargons.

Perhaps Lanham is right. Once we start thinking of jargon not as a collection of misplaced weeds but as a garden of metaphors, waiting to be dug up and repotted, we might just begin to get a new perspective, and spread a little beauty around the place. There are plenty of flowerbeds out there, and, who knows, by transplanting a weed or two and indulging in a little cross-pollinating, we may discover something new. Perhaps we need to take seriously the possibility that Gregor Mendel and Luther Burbank can be our role models as well as E.B. White and Lewis Thomas. Nothing immoral about that.

V.
The Editorial Temperament

The Editor as Seed Crystal

 n the theory that editors are just as narcissistic as the general population, and that we enjoy talking about ourselves just as much as failed actors and newly engaged couples, it's time to hold up the mirror to our sacred profession. The question is, what do we actually do?

First, since the glass doesn't lie, let's admit the truth. Despite the justifiable pride we may take in our craft, the living of an editor, like that of a book reviewer, is basically derivative. If it weren't for writers, most of us would be slinging hash instead of ink. Nonetheless, our profession does have standing of its own. There is some comfort, for example, in learning that—in English, at least—the verb *edit* did not come first, followed by the noun *editor*, as one might think. The *Oxford English Dictionary* (*OED*) (New York: Oxford University Press, 1986) reveals that *edit* is a back-formation from *editor*. (The *OED*'s first usage citation for *edit* is dated 1793; the first citation for *editor* is dated 1648.) This chronology does not necessarily mean that who we are takes precedence over what we do. It only revalidates the eternal truth that the ways of language are mysterious and there is no accounting for how some things get started.

A New Profession

Which brings us to point number two: Compared to a number of other professions, editing hasn't really been around all that long. It is only since the early 18th century that editors have been understood as persons who prepare the literary work of others for publication by a process of selection and revision. For about 150 years before that, *editor* was synonymous with *publisher*. Apparently, the assumption was that authors didn't need any help with their writing, only with the less savory task of getting it before the public. Thus, from the beginning, we editors have been in the mercantile mire. Knowledge of one's origins is a great antidote for professional hubris.

But like any useful new idea, the notion of an editor has caught on and gone from strength to strength. Like engineering, medicine, law, and theology, editing has proliferated specializations, continually rejustifying its precarious existence on the fringes of literature. There are acquisitions editors, line editors, copy editors, photo editors, technical editors, abstract editors, style editors, story editors, general editors, and to supervise them all, editors-in-chief. Thus, editors have become like doctors; you don't know without asking what any of them really does.

Dinner with the Queen

What most editors mostly do (we're talking here about the ones who do *not* get to take authors to lunch at Elaine's or the Four Seasons) is to read manuscripts with pencil in hand, correcting the errors of organization and presentation that may confuse a reader, offend the canons of standard English usage and grammar, or aggravate the ulcer of a printer.

If that sounds like a piece of cake, you either do not understand editing at all or have not been doing it very long. The main problem with our profession, as William Bridgewater, former editor-in-chief of Columbia University Press, has pointed out, is that it is a task without thoroughly set limits. In other words, in editing, as in dressing to go to dinner with the Queen, it's hard to know when you're "ready." And, truth to tell, more than anything else, what defines "ready" is that your manuscript, like your person at the palace, has a time beyond which, if it doesn't show up, everyone connected with the enterprise is embarrassed. You, most of all.

Message and Medium

My own view of editing is a little more exciting than that, however. For me, editing is an immersion in the endlessly fascinating chemistry of the English language. I have yet to meet the editor who is really as self-absorbed as my tongue-in-cheek introduction makes out. In truth, there is nothing editors care about so much as the endless possibilities for combination and recombination in language, and finding the right set of combinations for a particular manuscript. This passion is usually put in terms of the editor's responsibility to the author; what we really *must* care about is creating that arrangement of the author's words that best expresses the author's intention. What we seek is a kind of harmony, a crystallization in which message and medium merge.

When we do our jobs right, editors are like seed crystals. In chemistry, crystals are regular forms which seem to arise spontaneously and then replicate themselves in a stable manner. What sets this process off is a "seed crystal," which, when inserted into an assortment of molecules, brings those molecules together in a unique formation. Once the seed crystal is inserted, the molecules buzz around until, almost miraculously, they find the perfect arrangement to express exactly what they are. The result is maximum order and stability, in which all the molecules are organized in a way that leads to their continued existence. That's a job description for an editor if I ever heard one.

Hedgehogs and Foxes

s there such a thing as an "editorial mind?" Or, to put it another way, are there structures and habits of mind that are common to people in the editorial field? At one time I carelessly thought that editors were a mere psychological subtype—obsessive compulsives—who, like accountants, had managed to find a way to get society to reward their neurosis. Editors, I believed, were to language as orthodontists were to a bite: Neither could abide anything misplaced, whether modifier or incisor, and both took a perverse pleasure in the process of realignment. Taken to the extreme, this view of editors says they're all just a bunch of nitpickers—closet IRS examiners—who would rather mate with a goat than split an infinitive.

But charity has led me in another direction. Perhaps editors share not so much a neurosis as a particular cast of mind, a set of mental traits that describe how they create sense from the raw material of words. After some mild cogitation and at least one phone call to an editor friend to get a reality check, I have come up with what I hope is a reasonably accurate portrait of the kinds of minds editors have.

Aristotle and Isaiah Berlin

Editors are proof that Aristotle was right. Although editors come in all shapes, sizes, colors, genders, and dispositions, they tend to fall into two, and only two, broad categories when it comes to describing how they think. Some editors have synthetic minds. They look at any manuscript, whether a book or the copy for its dust jacket, in a way that sees the thing whole. Their minds are attuned to the vibrations of the major divisions (or fault lines); they resonate to the seismic undulations of overall logic, sequence of argument, major tempos, and structures. Given an alternative career as a lawyer, the synthetic editor would prefer sketching out the architecture of the case to finding the citations that would nail down decisive points of law.

Other editors have analytical minds. To them, editing a manuscript is a manual exercise in breakdown and reassembly, not unlike what an automobile mechanic goes through in diagnosing and fixing a car. The mechanic cares little for the car as a complete entity, being much more concerned with the fuel, electrical, exhaust, and cooling systems. Just so, the analytical editor does not see the whole manuscript, but a series of systems (syntax, punctuation, grammatical rules, forms of citation, etc.), each of which must be torn apart and rebuilt. The synthetic editor works from whole to parts, the analytical editor from parts to whole.

All this reminds me of the wonderful distinction the historian Isaiah Berlin made between what he called "the hedgehog and the fox." Great historical personages, said Berlin, are either one or the other, seldom both. Hedgehogs are imperial in their comprehension and articulation of grand historical visions and great ideas. Like Lenin, de Gaulle, and Washington, they see the big picture and take the long view. Foxes, on the other hand, are masters of the intricacies and subtleties of power tacticians rather than strategists. Aaron Burr, James Farley, and Cardinal Richelieu are examples of foxes; so are most political campaign managers.

You Can't Have It Both Ways

Although pure as types, these two kinds of editorial minds rarely occur unalloyed in the real world. The nature of editorial work itself makes that unlikely; the profession calls on editors both to get in the trenches of line editing and to ascend at least to the foothills of the Olympus where Zeuses like Maxwell Perkins and William Targ reside. I have met very few editors who are as good at one kind of editorial work as another. More to the point, I have met none who are equally proficient (or happy) at both. Not because of the all-too-human tendency to see the grass as greener, but because all good editors know what they're good at and how their own minds work—or should.

Which is as it ought to be. An editor who was both hedgehog and fox would be as formidable a combination in editing as Franklin Roosevelt was in politics. But no editorial shop worth working in could survive long without at least one of each. Editorial managers would do well, I think, to consider an open discussion among their staffs to figure out who is hedgehog and who is fox, and design a system of parceling out the work accordingly. It could save a lot of wasted motion—and talent.

The Encouragement of J.A.H. Murray

"very other author may aspire to praise; the lexicographer can only hope to escape reproach." Samuel Johnson's characterization of his calling applies as well to indexers, proofreaders, copy editors, and all of us who skewer our life's bread with blue pencils. It helps us to hear, now and again, the epic tales of the heroes and heroines of our vocation—how Kate L. Turabian could cow a full professor, or how Thomas Wolfe would never have made it out of Asheville had it not been for Maxwell Perkins.

The next time the risk of reproach threatens to overwhelm, try reading a bit of Elisabeth Murray's wonderful biography of Sir James A.H. Murray, her "Grandfather Dictionary," *Caught in the Web of Words* (New Haven, CT: Yale University Press, 1977). The card-carrying logophile will already know Murray as the greatest English lexicographer since Dr. Johnson. Murray edited THE dictionary, that work whose possession makes joining the Book-of-the-Month Club an excusable necessity.

In 1879, at age 42, Murray committed what he thought would be the next seven to ten years of his life to editing the (then called) *New English Dictionary on Historical Principles*. At his death 36 years later, the work had got as far as "S." The 12-volume *Oxford English Dictionary* (OED) was completed in 1928; a 4-volume supplement began appearing in 1972.

To read the story of Murray's life is to be at once delighted and inspired. To contemplate the magisterial scope of the *OED* and its importance to the English language is to be humbled. But after the reader hefts 15,487 quarto pages, glances through some half-million entries, and browses through the 1.5 million illustrative quotations selected from among nearly 6 million usage slips sent in by field readers—after all that—to discover that Murray edited *half of this himself* is to be stupefied.

The task of formulating even the typographical canons of a work such as the *OED*, let alone the mind-boggling problems of deciding what belonged in it or should be excluded, would be enough to induce a bad case of editorial hives. What distinguished Murray, and led to the ultimate success of his lexicon, was his absolute refusal to compromise his editorial standards. He preferred a production rate of zero to allowing less than his best effort to be printed. He never appeared to entertain the thought of "close enough is good enough." Though he engaged in repeated battles with the Delegates of the Oxford University Press, though he had to threaten resignation on several occasions, and though he had to face down one of the Victorian era's most formidable browbeaters, Benjamin Jowett, the Master of Balliol College, Murray remained unshakable. And he prevailed.

For Murray, editorial quality was an achievement purchased at the price of 36 years of 12-hour days. He wrote (longhand) an average of 20 to 30 letters a week to poets, writers, scientists, and authorities of all kinds inquiring about the meaning of words and terms. He and his staff ran down thousands of words to their Middle English roots, often producing trailblazing philological and linguistic scholarship in the process. He faced and overcame the hopelessness that often accompanied such tasks as sorting out verbs like "set," which occupies more than 18 pages of the dictionary and extends to 154 main divisions, the last of which (*set up*) has so many subdivisions that it exhausts the alphabet and repeats the letters down to *rr*.

Few today could aspire to, let alone match, his standard. But when the blue funk of frustration settles in, it is good to remember Murray. For him, the eternal editorial triangle of costs, time, and quality was never equilateral. Let the University Press rage about costs; let the public cool its heels forever waiting for the next fascicle; if it wasn't done right, it didn't go to the printer.

Team Editing

hy do so many editors work alone? Collaboration among writers is commonplace. Proofreading is done solo or in teams of two. Indeed, for many editorial managers, team proofing is the preferred method. Yet for editing, the opposite assumption seems to obtain: Usually we operate as if the preferred relationship between editor and document is one-on-one. Even when a single manuscript goes through a series of reviews by different editors, the editors line up single file. Assigning more than one editor at a time to a single manuscript is just not done—at least not often.

But why? The question is a bit more pointed for me as a result of recent experience and a current assignment. I have a contract to edit (and, where necessary, rewrite) the final report of a national commission. I got the job because three years ago I worked with the report's author on a similar study. We have flattered ourselves that its success was rooted (at least in part) in our own ability to work together. Over several months we had partly devised and partly stumbled into a division of labor that made so much sense and was so enjoyable and challenging that it seemed worth trying to recreate.

Our teamwork succeeds because each of us brings particular strengths to the enterprise. My partner has a gift for being able to see the document whole at all times; I enjoy some success at wordsmithing and sentence-craft. He penetrates easily to the heart of ideas; I have an intuition about "what works" that satisfies the taste and sensibilities of both of us. I have a broader knowledge of usage than he; his merciless blue pencil is ever ready when my black one acquires a mind of its own. Because neither of us is exceptionally knowledgeable about the specifics of publications style, we simply keep a manual handy to resolve thorny issues. Or, we make things up as we go along, keeping track of idiosyncratic decisions that could trip us up later. Each of us, I think, has a good ear.

In the beginning, what enabled our team editing relationship to work was a kind of serendipitous complementarity. But what keeps it working is a thorough knowledge of one another's strengths and weaknesses as editors and a trust in one another's judgment. That, and a deliberate suppression of ego. We both enjoy the give and take because it produces results. Actually seeing the drafts improve is reinforcing. Rarely does one of us have so great an investment in our work that he will not bow to the other's strongly felt opinion about how to make a sentence or paragraph better. Frequently, we simply "trade," as in "You won the last argument; this one is mine."

I find it hard to believe that this kind of relationship cannot be constructed deliberately, either by an editorial manager who understands his or her staff, or by two or more editors who are sufficiently self-aware to be able to seek their natural complements. Team editing would be a particularly strong editorial approach to large-scale projects, where two heads really are better than one. Each can serve as the other's natural goad and corrective.

In the end, if the project goes well and the team jells, the two can learn to create a kind of synergy. Interacting with the manuscript, they become the yeast, creating the fermentation that the lone editor seldom knows.

VI.
Words

"Confusibles"

ertain words remind me of a bad marriage. They ought to get divorced, but somehow they can't break away from one another. Like Siamese cats, they seem to travel in pairs although they occasionally appear in a threesome. Sometimes they share an etymological history, rather like feuding cousins who claim the same great-grandfather. Usually they have the same number of syllables and sound similar or alike to the un-tuned ear. H.W. Fowler called them "pairs and snares"; John Simon calls them "sibling rivals"; Adrian Room, the English lexicographer, calls them "confusibles." (See his wonderful paperback, *Room's Dictionary of Confusibles* (New York: Methuen, Inc., 1979), or its enlarged version, *Dictionary of Confusing Words and Meanings* (Boston: Routledge & Kegan Paul, 1985).)

All of us have a confusible or two in the closet of our everyday language. Some say *affect* when they mean *effect*, or vice versa. Some say *capacity* when they mean *capability* (or v.v.). Even President Carter said *flaunt* once at a press conference when he meant *flout*.

We all stumble. Is a witty saying an *epitaph* or an *epigram*? Does your jolly old Uncle Ned *chortle* or *chuckle*—or both? But when is he doing which? Does a *sensual* woman (man) excite you? Or is that *sensuous*?

To be a really good confusible, a set of words has to meet some pretty rigorous standards. First, the words ought to be homophones (*chord/cord*, *sum/some*), or nearly so (*fraction/faction*, *fervid/fervent*), although sometimes only parts of the words are phonetically similar (*discerning/discriminating*). Second, the words should be the same part of speech, as with *triumphant* and *triumphal*, which are both adjectives.

But the main trouble with a really good confusible is that its words huddle together under the same semantic umbrella.

Take *denote* and *connote*, both of which have to do with meaning or signifying. The difference between them is that *denote* means to indicate a thing directly, the way a gauge denotes the pressure in a boiler, whereas *connote* means to add something to the literal meaning; e.g., as *hearth*, which denotes the floor of a fireplace or its surrounding area, and connotes warmth and security as well.

Words like *gorilla* and *guerrilla* don't qualify as true confusibles, even though both can be dangerous in the jungle. They are etymologically worlds and centuries apart. *Gorilla* is an allegedly African word, preserved via Greek, meaning "hairy man" "guerrilla" is the Spanish diminutive of *guerra*—"war."

Here are some fairly common confusibles. See if you can *distinguish/discriminate* them before reading ahead for the answers. If you can distinguish/discriminate five or more of the pairs, you get a "U" for Usage:

> *avenge/revenge; delegate/relegate; deplore/deprecate; licentious/ lascivious/lecherous; nauseous/nauseated; notable/noticeable; persistence/perseverance; pervade/permeate; presume/assume; repel/repulse.*

> *avenge/revenge:* These words were once interchangeable, but today *avenge* suggests legitimate vindication ("'Vengeance is mine,' saith the Lord"), whereas *revenge* arises from baser motives.

> *delegate/relegate:* To *delegate* a task is merely to hand it over; to *relegate* it, however, is to place it in a lower position or order of priority.

> *deplore/deprecate:* If you *deplore* a thing you regret it. *Deprecate* is the word people used before *putdown* entered our vocabulary. It means "to belittle."

> *licentious/lascivious/lecherous:* All three have to do with lewdness or lust. *Licentious* acts are characterized by license, i.e., they lack moral restraint. *Lascivious* means a predisposition toward lewd or lustful behavior. But *lecherous* means actually given over to grab and tickle and whatever else. Together, they create a direct progression: licentiousness gets rid of the inhibitions, lasciviousness provides the disposition to act, lecherousness is the nittygritty.

> *nauseous/nauseated:* This pair is a personal favorite, since almost everyone gets it wrong, thus affording me (and now you) a chance to show off. Something *nauseous* has the capability to induce nausea. *Nauseated* is the way people feel when they encounter something nauseous. People who say "Chinese food makes me nauseous" should say

nauseated. They are *nauseous* only if they throw up and make their dinner companions *nauseated*.

notable/noticeable: A *notable* difference is one worth noticing; a *noticeable* difference is merely conspicuous.

persistence/perseverance: Persistence, as any upper-class Englishman can tell you, is dogged resolve. It is the interior attitude of which the exterior manifestation is often *perseverance,* i.e., continuing in the same path despite difficulties.

pervade/permeate: When someone closes a window and puts a match to a pile of oily rags, the smell soon *pervades*—it is soon present throughout the room. If that smell is to make its way to the next room, however, it has to *permeate,* or pass through, a barrier.

presume/assume: If you *assume* I'll come to your party, it's because you have already made up your mind that I will, or because I have some obligation to show up. But if you *presume* I'll come, you're taking me for granted and will be surprised if I don't come. And that is presumptuous.

repel/repulse: The unwelcome advances of a masher upon a well-bred young lady may be either *repelled* (warded off) or *repulsed* (driven back). If he tries to press the matter further, he's sure to be called *repulsive, repugnant,* or *repellent.* But which of the three he is called will depend not only on how vigorously obnoxious he has been, but on how carefully she chooses her words.

If you still find yourself unsure of when to use *farther* or *further, infer* or *imply, uninterested* or *disinterested,* don't despair. Even Arthur Miller showed his clay feet in "Death of a Salesman," when he has Biff say to his father, Willy, "What am I doing in an office, making a contemptuous, beggin' fool of myself?"

What he meant to say, of course, was *contemptible.*

"And"

arlier in this book, I suggested that editors should encourage writers to spend time looking up the words they use in the *Oxford English Dictionary* (*OED*). A further suggestion was that this practice would be particularly useful for the commonest words in English. On the principle that one should never hand out advice that one is unwilling to take, I spent some time perusing the *OED* entry for *and*. It has a venerable and interesting pedigree.

A Little History

Like most of the little words (*the, of, but, for, in*), *and* has been around for a long time in one form or another. Although most of us know it is a simple connective and coordinating conjunction, *and* began its life in the Indo-European family of languages as a preposition, expressing the idea of opposition, juxtaposition, or antithesis. As it made its way into the Teutonic languages from which English eventually arose, the meaning of *and* shifted to encompass the idea of mutuality or relationship. In Old English, *and* was used prepositionally to express the idea of local (before, in the presence of) or logical (along with, besides, in addition to) relation; nouns governed by *and* were placed in the dative case.

The first recorded instance of the most common use of *and* we know in English—that of a simple connective—occurs in Old English about the year 700. The (again, first recorded) use of *and* to express the idea of continuous repetition appears about the year 1000 in a surviving text of the Gospel of Mark, where Jesus sends out his disciples to preach: "agan hi sendan twam and twam" (he sent them out two by two). The idea of expressing a difference of quality between things of the same class is first written down in 1569 in a sample of special moral pleading offered by Kingesmyll in his *Conflict with Satan*: "There is a sinne and a sinne: (there is) much oddes between the committing of sinnes in the reprobate and in the elect." The use of *and* as a coordinating conjunction for clauses or sentences is first recorded in 855 in the *Old English Chronicle*.

Since its earliest appearances, *and* has added a number of nuances to its meaning. For example, *and* can be used to introduce a consequence or result ("A few paces from the back door and I came upon the well"). It can be used to add an explanatory amplification ("We and we alone are responsible"). *And* can also be used to connect two verbs, the latter of which would logically be in the infinitive form, especially after *try, go, send, come:* ("John will go and do it").

Usage

Despite its commonness and simplicity, *and* can get surprisingly tricky. One of the most common faults editors encounter occurs when writers muddy the distinction between the simple connective use of *and* and its coordinating use. This is what H.W. Fowler, in *A Dictionary of Modern English Usage* (New York: Oxford University Press, 1983) calls "bastard enumeration," exemplified in a sentence like "He was pleased that most of his guests were happy, convivial and had a good sense of humor." The problem is that the writer has tried to get *and* to play both connective and coordinating roles. The result is a lack of grammatical parallelism. There are two corrections possible: (1) make all elements parallel by using *and* throughout: "He was pleased that his guests were happy and convivial and had a good sense of humor; or (2) break the clauses with a comma and add *and that* to introduce the second clause: "He was pleased that his guests were happy and convivial, and that they had a good sense of humor."

A different sort of issue arises in a stylistic device that is becoming more common. (Do these things go in cycles?) It is the practice of dropping the *and* between the penultimate and ultimate terms in enumerations: "The candidate promised to reduce the deficit, taxes, unemployment." This is a form of the rhetorical device called asyndeton, in which conjunctions are suppressed to heighten the effect. Fowler suggests that the trend may be attributed to the influence of headline writing, where *and* becomes superfluous, or to the desire to suggest that the enumeration is not exhaustive. Whatever the intention, it is a non-use of *and* that editors ought to discourage. As with all effects, overuse quickly becomes affectation.

And/Or

One of the most disagreeable uses of *and* is in the legalism *and/or*. Lawyers are well paid to protect their clients from every possible contingency and circumstance that could possibly harm them;

hence, they tend to insert *and/or* into every situation where either might convey the meaning; the other is appended "just in case." But what is permissible in a contract is impermissible in polite company, or is just plain laziness in writing. The trouble with *and/or* is that it evades the responsibility every writer has to create proper sentence structure. Most of the time *or* will do quite nicely. If a sentence like "Most people go to the mall to browse and/or do a little shopping" were written "with browsing or shopping in mind," sensible readers would understand that some browse, some shop, and some do both. Nothing said or implied prevents all three possibilities. The same usually holds true if *and* is chosen. "X and/or Y" can also be rendered as "either X or Y, or both," to cover those situations where distinctions are important; writers should make good use of the construction. Where it doesn't work, rewrite the sentence.

And when it comes to whether a writer can begin a sentence with *and*, we like to quote Wilson Follett, in *Modern American Usage: A Guide*. (New York: Hill & Wang, 1966): "A prejudice lingers from the days of schoolmarmish rhetoric that a sentence should not begin with *and*. The supposed rule is without foundation in grammar, logic, or art." Take that, Miss Thistlebottom.

Nonce Words, Vogue Words, and Whatchamacallits

ost dictionaries define a *nonce word* as one coined "for the nonce," that is, for a particular occasion, presumably never to be used again. There is, of course, a paradox hidden in the definition, which, if taken strictly and logically, would mean that the very discussion of a nonce word removed it from its own category.

That logical dead end aside, *American Heritage* cites *mileconsuming*, as in the following fragment from Faulkner: "the wagon beginning to fall into its slow and mileconsuming clatter." William and Mary Morris, in *Harper Dictionary of Contemporary Usage* (New York: Harper & Row, 1985) offer the charming example of a nonce word arising from the centennial celebration of Lincoln, Illinois. There the townspeople minted a wooden, commemorative coin valued at 7.5 cents. Since it was worth less than a dime but more than a nickel, they called it a *dickel*. The word had not been used before nor has it been used since. (Except, of course, by the Morrises and now by me. See the last sentence of the previous paragraph.)

Euphonic criteria excepted, not all nonce words are as agreeable as *dickel*. The Morrises also report on a linguistic researcher, one Sarah Gudschinsky, to whom they (incorrectly) attribute the term *glottochronology*, a coinage to describe a technique for establishing the age of words. As with most nonce words, the world is not much the better for it.

Vogue Words

Nonce words with potential tend to move to the status of vogue words, thence quickly downward to the debased coinage of full cliché. Examples of vogue words abound: *tracking (on); parameter; impact (v.); hype; mega-* (choose your own suffix); (choose your own prefix) *-gate, -aholic; juice* (in the sense of "power" or "clout"). And William Safire, in *On Language* (New York: Avon Books,

1981) has censured the political scientists who have labeled voters *microdecisionmakers.*

Vogue words are to speakers and writers what the herd instinct is to lemmings. The sudden explosion of these words into print and cocktail party conversation is a sure sign that the front-runners have already plunged over the linguistic edge. As H.W. Fowler (who coined the term) points out, many vogue words owe their ubiquity simply to the fact that most of us can't resist showing off; we thus tend to get the kind of language we deserve.

Whatchamacallits

Lately, though, I have been bedeviled by a different kind of nonce word, which I have never seen discussed. These words are not used once but are used only as part of a singular expression. Far from aspiring to the dubious stature of vogue words, they have no aspirations at all; they can't seem to break out of the unique context in which they occur. They give birth to no similes or metaphors. Indeed, they are linguistic parasites, unable to detach themselves from their host words to find semantic sustenance elsewhere.

The clearest example I can think of is *amok.* This word is borrowed from Malay; in that language it means "furious attack" and can presumably be used in a variety of contexts. In English, however, we say only "run amok," nothing else. Another such word is *dudgeon,* meaning "a sullen, angry, indignant humor." But why are all dudgeons "high"? Perhaps one might issue a tongue-in-cheek warning about a wimp in "low dudgeon," but I have never seen such. There are others. *Wend* means to "proceed or go along," but is a semantic cripple without its unfailing sequel "(his, her, its) way." You need "arms" to use the word *akimbo;* you can only be "taken" *aback; recuse* now almost always requires a reflexive pronoun, as in judges and lawyers who recuse themselves on grounds of conflict of interest.

English is such a plastic language that I am puzzled by the infertility of these relatively common terms. Why can they not give life to some other expressions? And how should we refer to this phenomenon?

Perhaps readers of *The Editorial Eye* newsletter can come to my rescue—in two respects. First, I am interested in extending this list. If you can think of other such single-instance usages, I would appreciate learning of them. Second, I wonder if readers can come up with a term that covers this sort of word. If so, you will have created a word that can be used in only one way: to discuss the class of words for which it is the denominating member. But could it logically be used to discuss itself? (If such conundrums delight you, you're probably the kind who reads Bertrand Russell, Douglas Hofstadter, or Raymond Smullyan for relaxation.)

Author's Note: A reader offered *sololocutions* as an excellent term for words that are used only one way. Other examples of sololocutions include *loggerheads*, which invariably appears with *at; betwixt*, which never appears without *between; the nines*, which are always *dressed to; durance*, which is always *vile; lucre*, which is always *filthy; fettle*, which is always *fine;* and *shrift*, for which there is no medium or long, only *short*.

"Very"

ne of the best ways to quit smoking is to announce to all your friends that you're doing it. That way, every time you light up, there is someone around to make you feel guilty. That's the theory behind the policy I'm announcing on the use of *very*.

I use *very* too much. I know this to be a fact because virtually every time someone edits something I've written, it comes back with at least one *very* stricken out. So let's get this on the record: I'm quitting. Or maybe not quitting entirely, but at least launching a campaign to keep my own readers from becoming the equivalent of passive smokers, forced to breathe the invisible fumes of this wispy modifier.

One way smokers who hope to become nonsmokers get that way is by reminding themselves of all the nasty things that cigarettes do to their bodies. Well, then, what are some of the nasty things *very* can do to your writing?

For one thing, *very* tends to weaken the art of clear and accurate description. Its basic use is as an intensifier, making an adjective, adverb, or participial more of what it is already (*very angry, very pleased*). But this use ought to strike the careful writer (and editor) as a form of laziness. After all, aren't words like *furious* or *enraged* more clear or accurate than *very angry*? Isn't it more descriptive to say *gratified, delighted,* or *elated* than *very pleased*?

Another bad thing *very* does to writing is a kind of overkill: Writers use it in a vain attempt to strengthen already strong words. A "very adamant refusal" might better be expressed as a "foot-stamping refusal"; a "very polished performance" might be better rendered as "a burnished performance." The use of *very* in such contexts is self-defeating; instead of intensifying the image, the writer succeeds only in dulling it. I like Theodore Bernstein's example of this fault, which is a kind of conceptual pun. A writer, he says, "may write, 'Hemingway's prose is very lean and very strong,' not realizing he would express his thought more forcefully if he wrote 'Hemingway's prose is lean and strong.'" In other words, if the intent of using *very* is to strengthen the force of the writing, the writer should reexamine the choice of words before piling on a *very*. After all, when you get down to it, what is the difference between a *great man* and a *very great man*, other than the suspicion that the latter may have a skeleton or two hanging about the odd closet?

Some grammarians and authorities on usage make much of the contention that *very*, which was originally a full-fledged adjective (e.g., the Nicene Creed refers to Jesus Christ as "very God of very God"), has become a half-fledged adverb. *Very* is half-fledged because it ought to be able to modify a verb, yet we cannot say "Phyllis very loves Athelstan." The argument is carried further by the point that *very* may properly be used to modify adjectives denoting quality (*very smart*) but not participial adjectives denoting actions (*very educated*). The trouble, as Bernstein points out, arises when the participial begins wandering away from the verb that gave it birth and starts "feeling" more like an adjective (*interested, pleased, tired, neglected*).

Some will contend that *very* as an intensifier is allowable as long as *much* is used with it ("The spies were very much to be commended for their skulduggery"), but this argument, too, runs aground on the shoals of the adjective/participle continuum. Using *very* with *interested* works as well as or better than *very much* ("Wilfred was very interested in Samoan cuisine") because *interested* has a strong adjectival quality. But *very* does not work as well with a participle that retains its verbal quality ("Rodney and Alicia are very divorced").

In the end, *very* winds up being a prop for a word or sentence that can get along well without it, a bit of baggage that weighs things down, or too dull a knife to split a semantic hair. Most of the time the best policy is to do without it. Maybe if we all used it less, it might get a little stronger. In the meantime, I'm *very* determined to swear off.

Words for Edit

ost of us think we have a fairly clear idea of what the verb *edit* means—until we start to think about it. A little reflection and a good thesaurus can turn that assumption into a quivering jelly of uncertainty in less time than it takes to insert an em-dash.

My favorite thesaurus (Laurence Urdang's complete revision of *The Synonym Finder* originally compiled by J.I. Rodale and republished by the Rodale Press, 1978) offers 31 formal synonyms for *edit*, 4 informal ones (*prep, delete, blue-pencil, clean up*), and 2 contextually limited to television (*blip* and *bleep*). Herewith is a closer look at some of them, with a view to a lesson on the role of synonymy.

Editing in General

At a minimum, sorting out synonyms for our daily labor can be a bracing, even ego-inflating exercise because it brings editors face to face with how versatile we are. First, there are certain words for *edit* that give a general idea of what editors do. These are the "re-" words like *revise, rewrite,* and *rephrase* that describe our broad cultural role as literary nannies. After all, we *are* hired to tidy up after messy writers who can't quite remember where this or that mark of punctuation goes, who commit the occasional mixaphor, or whose exuberance occasionally gets in the way of clarity. Another word that belongs among the synonyms-general for edit is *amend*. In addition to meaning "making changes," *amend* imparts the qualitative sense that *edit* sometimes carries, i.e., changes made with a view to making a manuscript better.

Once that Pandora's box is open, the synonyms for *edit* fall into three groups, each related to a different kind of editorial task. As noted elsewhere in this collection ("Hedgehogs and Foxes"), editors tend to have one of two kinds of minds, analytic or synthetic, which suit them for two different kinds of editorial work. It should come as no surprise, then, that a large number of synonyms for *edit* fall into these two categories.

Analysis and Synthesis

To edit with an analytic turn of mind means to look at a manuscript as a series of specific systems (punctuation, syntax, style rules, usage, grammatical rules, forms of citation, and the like). Thus, analytical synonyms for *edit* include

♦ *modify*—to change slightly or partially in character

♦ *correct*—to remove errors from or bring into conformity to a standard

♦ *emend*—to correct or improve

♦ *redact*—to arrange in proper form or condition

♦ *annotate*—to provide explanatory notes

♦ *delete*—to take out.

To edit with a synthetic turn of mind is to do the opposite: to look at a manuscript as a whole, seeing its structure, its logic, the progression of its line of argument or development, and the relation of the parts to the whole. Synonyms for edit in this sense include

♦ *select*—to choose by some criterion or special quality

♦ *compile*—to compose a book of materials from various sources

♦ *prepare*—to make ready a manuscript for publication.

A third set of synonyms involves the strongest application of values to the material at hand. These are the synonyms that dance around the dangerous bonfire of censorship, or that apply in contexts where editing means, in effect, advancing some particular cause or ideology. This group of synonyms includes such words as

♦ *expurgate*—to remove objectionable passages from a manuscript

♦ *expunge*—to remove completely

♦ *abridge*—to reduce in scope or shorten

♦ *bowdlerize*—to remove passages considered offensive (after Thomas Bowdler, an English editor who published an expurgated version of Shakespeare in 1818).

The many words for *edit* describe the many tasks, indeed, the many perspectives a good editor must have. They also show the potential pitfalls of the profession. It is all too easy for editors to bow down in worship before the great god Image, particularly those among us who work in public relations and corporate communications. We need to be particularly aware, for example, when the shades of meaning for *edit* begin to shift gradually away from the purely mechanical and analytical and toward the substantive, the synthetic, and the qualitative. It is but a short journey from "clearer" language to "better" language that is deemed better because it is less objectionable. And it is a quick journey from being objectionable because of inaccuracies to being objectionable because the truth is unpleasant.

In English there are no true (i.e., exact) synonyms. Their role is to provide nuance. Often that means bridging the distance between daylight and dark by providing the subtle shades of twilight. Editors need to remember that.

The Trouble with "Only"

s a general rule, "write the way you talk" is a fairly sensible admonition. Most of us speak grammatically most of the time, and when we don't, we usually know it or our friends make allowances. Writing the way you talk also tends to keep you from wandering off into the stratospheres of jargon or losing your way in the labyrinth of convoluted syntax. The Resident Teenager, I am happy to say, learned this lesson recently when he discovered that his English paper didn't have to sound like a textbook to get a good mark.

But there are times when writing the way you talk can get you into trouble. Take the way we (or perhaps I ought not to create accomplices—let's say I) sometimes use the word *only* in writing.

Only is an extremely useful modifier, but deceptive. The meaning of the word itself contains a drive toward exclusivity (it is derived from *one*). Among its several meanings as an adjective, it is used to express the idea of "alone of its kind," as in "She is my only wife." As an adverb, it is used to express the idea of "and no other," as in "Only the seniors made the trip to New York." Even its colloquial usage expresses a sense of being exclusionary or contrary, as when we say, "I'd have gone, only it rained."

The trouble *only* creates arises when its meaning is contradicted by its placement in the sentence. If we say, "The lamp can only be seen if it is lit," a sentence that most of us would readily speak, we are on the verge of solecism because what we intend to say is "The lamp can be seen only if it is lit."

And to be sure, teachers of writing and editing never tire of showing their students how sentences can be variously construed by inserting *only* at every possible point in a sentence, e.g.:

"I hit the ball with the bat yesterday."

"She told me that she loved me."

"My uncle, shouting invectives, was arrested."

Each of these sentences is capable of as many (often wildly vary-ing) interpretations as there are points of insertion. Such lessons are all to the good because they make us—writers and editors all—sen-sitive to where we are putting such intrinsically powerful modifiers.

But it is possible to get carried away with all this, and I wonder if it isn't time to chew on the other end of the stick for a while. Theodore Bernstein points out in *The Careful Writer: A Modern Guide to English Usage* (New York: Atheneum, 1965) that there are "nor-mal" positions for *only*, not always as close as possible to the word it qualifies. These normal placements sound fine to the ear, but if we correct them in writing, they seem awkward and contrived, as in "What we are witnessing can only be called a revolution." Here, *only* should properly precede *a revolution*, but it comes across as pedantic.

Another "abnormal" sentence can result when we correct sen-tences in which *only*, in effect, modifies the entire sentence: "He only thought he was being helpful." Here *only* does not really modify *thought;* the intention is to attach the limiting sense of *only* to the whole sentence.

This use of *only* is similar to another pointed out by Bernstein, as when *only* is used to limit a statement being made: "The manage-ment will honor the blue tickets only if they are presented on Tues-days." The sentence is unambiguous, but is improved only marginally (if at all) by moving *only* to a position between *will* and *honor*.

The great H.W. Fowler, somewhat surprisingly, comes down thumpingly on the opposite side of the barricades from the zealots on this one. He says that partisans of the view that *only* should always be positioned exactly where it eliminates all ambiguity, instead of where natural speech puts it, have "more zeal than discre-tion." He goes on:

> But this tendency [that languages have toward a natural sifting out of their own illogicalities and inaccuracies of expression] has its bad as well as its good effects; the pedants who try to forward it when the illogicality is only apparent or the inaccuracy of no importance are turning English into an exact science or an automatic machine. *[A Dictionary of Modern English Usage]*

Just because an orthodoxy has sprung up for the placement of *only* does not mean heterodoxy constitutes heresy. To the statement "He only died a week ago," the pedant will reply, "What do you mean, 'only' died? Could he have done anything more singular or final?" But for Fowler, the sentence (which is his) needs no better defense than that this is the way most of us would say it. Where the risk of misunderstanding is minimal, departure from the natural is uncalled for.

So, by all means, let's be careful where we put our *onlies*. Only let's try to keep from getting uptight about it.

VII.
Stuff
And
Nonsense

The Dictionary Dodge

here's a potato chip company whose advertising slogan used to be "Bet You Can't Eat Just One." I have a parallel problem with dictionaries. Every time I open one, whatever the reason, I rarely stop looking when I find what I went after. To me, dictionaries are like Disney World; they were made to wander around in.

Along that line, I have always thought that the most important characteristic of any good dictionary was not its accuracy or comprehensiveness, but whether it could keep you from doing more useful work. Never having subjected that prejudice to scientific scrutiny, and having recently wakened with a terminal case of the blaaahs, I devised an experiment. My hypothesis was that any single page of my dictionary, chosen at random, could keep me interested long enough to waste at least an hour.

I took my desk dictionary (a scarred *American Heritage*, 1969), let it fall open at random, and timed how long I could avoid other activity. Unfortunately, I was able to remain on p. 846 for only 27 minutes. But that's not the whole story.

Play by the Rules

There are some rules for doing this sort of thing that ought to be mentioned before the results are fully reported. *Rule One:* You have to stick with your page. Abandoning it just because it happens to be one on which all the words begin with the same prefix is cheating. *Rule Two:* As a warm-up you have to run through all the entries quickly and see how many words you either know or recognize. If "Words Known" exceed "Words Unknown," you may be headed for trouble. But don't despair; there are plenty of byways to explore. A more rigorous version of Rule Two is to substitute being able to give a fair definition of the word instead of just being able to recognize it. This rule may also be called the Humility Rule. *Rule Three:* Save the longest entry until last, sort of like the maraschino cherry in a manhattan, unless you don't like maraschino cherries or don't drink, in which case it's OK to read the longest entry first. *Rule Four:*

Note-taking is forbidden. There's no point in using a dictionary to waste time if you're going to get fanatical about it.

From "moll" to "monad"

Page 846 runs from *moll* to *monad*. The most engaging (and longest) entry, the kind for which the *American Heritage* has been justly praised, is for *moment*. Eight main definitions are presented, the first two of which seem to contradict one another in sense: "1. a brief, indefinite period of time," and "2. a specific point in time, especially the present time." Alice's question to Humpty Dumpty comes to mind: "The question is whether you can make a word mean so many different things." Humpty Dumpty's response, of course, is probably the definitive commentary on all usage: "The question is, who is to be the master—that's all."

Definitions 7 and 8 of *moment* are special to physics and statistics. One of the two from physics I could understand: ("the rotation produced in a body when force is applied; torque"). The other one reminded me of why I majored in history. The one from statistics was, to be sure, as succinct as a dictionary definition should be: ("the expected value of a positive integral power of a random variable"). Having abandoned anything to do with what I call "the quantitative morass" when I parted company with second-year algebra, I did not tarry long with this lexicographical pearl, except to wonder about the connection between a "positive integral power" and the Latin root *momentum*, meaning a "movement."

There follows a whole paragraph of synonyms, ranked according to duration in comparison with *moment*. *Moment* and *minute*, used informally, are regarded as of interchangeable length. An *instant* is shorter than either and also carries connotations of haste and urgency. *Second* may be used specifically or loosely as the equivalent of *instant*. *Trice, jiffy*, and *flash*, however, while they are of approximately the same duration as *instant* and may imply haste, need not imply urgency. I have a hard time believing that a *flash* isn't a lot faster than a *jiffy*, however.

Proof of the Hypothesis

The most interesting word on the page (an interesting word is a nonscientific word I don't know) was *momus*, a word particularly appropriate for editors because it derives from *Momus*, the god of blame and ridicule in Greek mythology. A *momus* is a carping faultfinder.

Momus was a delightful find because it inspired me to look up the god of which this word is the eponym, first in Bulfinch's *Mythology* (New York: Modern Library, 1970), then in Willard Espy's delightful book on eponyms, *O Thou Improper, Thou Uncommon Noun* (out of print). And with that, I shot the rest of the morning.

Q.E.D.

"Let's Have Some New Clichés"

'm waiting for the other shoe to drop. It goes with the territory. She's marching to a different drummer. It really blew my mind. That's just the tip of the iceberg.

It's time we starting swearing off certain expressions before our minds rot. It isn't that these ways of putting things weren't originally useful, clever, or apt; it's just that they retain all the sparkle of six-day-old Perrier.

I figure that with some imagination, we can exterminate a few of the little beasties and raise a new crop. In the words of Samuel Goldwyn, "Let's have some new clichés." Herewith is a list of some reigning clichés, with suggested heirs apparent.

REIGNING CLICHÉ	HEIR APPARENT
can of worms	sack of spaghetti
circle the wagons	heads in, buns out
down the tubes	juiced, sluiced, and traduced
fell between the cracks	got thrown out with the junk mail
fun and games	trivial pursuits
good news/bad news	December two-five/April one-five
laundry list	dance card
come on like gangbusters	do a J. Edgar
media event	channel fodder
moment of truth	time to stab, jump, or get gored
perfectly clear	Milhousian
since sliced bread	since Adam gave up gardening
stay tuned	keep your Walkman on
take it from the top	from Egg #1
wearing two hats	doing a Jekyll/Hyde

Divertimenti

ord lovers are surely living in the best of all possible times. With each new visit of the postperson (who brings the direct mail), or with each hour killed in a bookstore, there's a tempting new diversion: Someone has built yet another prism through which to refract the language. We suffer from an embarrassment of riches; these books are coming out faster than they can be read, and that is no mean feat, considering the fact that most can be polished off in an hour or so.

I have four of these books at my elbow, all acquired recently, each begging me to stop what I'm doing and pay attention to it. The only thing to do is to make them what I am doing, i.e., to write about them, so I can clear my desk and you can have a good excuse to clutter up yours. Here are four more books you can't afford but will probably buy two of.

Sniglets

Sniglets are words that don't appear in the dictionary but should. Rich Hall and his friends have helpfully collected quite a few of them, which the Macmillan people have graciously published (1986).* Most sniglets are portmanteau words, in which two meanings are stuffed into the same word to capture both ideas—for example, Walter Winchell's famous *infanticipating* (for pregnant). Thus, if you are the type who always passes over licorice jellybeans, you will be delighted to know that you are *antalixic*. If you want to find those single socks that disappear in the laundry, just send their mates off to the *hozone* to look for them. Writers and editors can add *erdu* to their lexicon; it is the leftover accumulation of rubber particles made by erasing mistakes.

---

*Mr. Hall knows a good thing when he comes across it. Since *Sniglets* came out, there have been five follow-ons, not to mention the calendars, T-shirts, and what all.

No Uncertain Terms

This word book is actually useful. Mark and Diane Dittrick have put together a word collection that helps people sort out the differences between seemingly simple names of things that all of us think we know but regularly confuse or misuse. Most of us cannot tell the difference (or may not even know the difference) between a *spire* and a *steeple* (a spire is the pointed roof of a church tower; a steeple is the tower plus the spire). The difference between a *cougar*, a *mountain lion*, and a *puma* is nonexistent; all are the same feline. But how about *dock, wharf*, and *pier; gorge* and *canyon; cyclone* and *tornado; marsh, bog*, and *swamp*? *No Uncertain Terms* (New York: Facts on File Publications, 1984) tells all, and if you think you know it all already, better read pp. 104-05, where you'll learn the difference between an *egoist*, an *egotist*, and a *narcissist*.

The Book of Similes

Readers of detective fiction know that Raymond Chandler, creator of Philip Marlowe, could spit out similes faster than a bishop could run from a brothel. He and dozens of other comparison-minded writers, celebrities, and politicians appear in this fascinating collection by Robert Baldwin and Ruth Paris (New York: Methuen, Inc., 1982). All have been chosen for their wit and perception and arranged alphabetically for easy reference. Here's a sampling that should appeal to writers and editors:

dull as a widder-woman's axe.—*Anon.* (Ozark-USA)

clear as the inside of a blackberry pie.—*Anon.*

critics are like eunuchs in a harem: They know how it's done, they've seen it done every day, but they're unable to do it themselves.—*Brendan Behan*

busier than a man with $400 and a thirst.—*Damon Runyon*

A few of Chandler's best:

all the originality and drive of a split fingernail

dead as a pickled walnut

shorter than a bargain-counter shirt

as easy to spot as a kangaroo in a dinner jacket

laughing like a hen having the hiccups

gaudy as a chiropractor's chart

the dignity of an intoxicated dowager.

Words

Words are what it's all about, and Paul Dickson has written a "connoisseur's collection of old and new, weird and wonderful, useful and outlandish" (New York: Dell, 1983). Dickson characterizes himself as a compulsive word collector, who confesses that "I have spent time that could have been used increasing the GNP compiling totally useless but altogether satisfying collections including 315 phobias and 74 gums" (p. 1).

This book attracted a lot of attention when it came out, largely because a lot of reviewers were entranced by the fact that it contains 2,231 synonyms for *drunk*. But that's like developing a fascination for Meryl Streep because she has the longest hair of any working actress. The treasures of *Words* far exceed a feat of synonymy. On p. 192, for example, Dickson offers Dr. Wilfred Funk's list of the most beautiful words in English, some chosen for meaning, some for euphony. Among others, it includes *fawn, anemone, murmuring, lullaby, cerulean, gossamer, oleander, luminous,* and *asphodel* (a flower). Language oddity freaks who are sure that no English word contains a double y should know that Dickson has found one: *snarleyyow,* in Webster II.

Dickson has some sniglets of his own, a short list of 45 words created as a kind of defense mechanism for inhabiting the last quarter of the 20th century. Some of my favorites: *anthonize,* giving the public what it does not want, as in the Susan B. Anthony dollar coin; *Cosellian,* the highest level of smugness and self-certainty, an eponym of Howard Cosell; *fabricist,* one who discriminates against others on the basis of their clothes and the labels in them; and *translute,* a portmanteau of translate and convolute, used to designate a translation that changes the meaning entirely, as when President Carter's "I want to understand your desires for the future" came out as "I desire the Poles carnally."

For Abecdearians—Alpha to Omega *and* ABC et Cetera

Two delightful books that will provide hours of fascination and diversion for any writer or editor are the twin volumes written by Alexander and Nicholas Humez, *Alpha to Omega: The Life and Times of the Greek Alphabet* and *ABC et Cetera: The Life and Times of the Roman Alphabet* (Boston: David R. Godine, Publisher, 1983, 1987). More than just an explanation of the letters themselves, each provides a window on the cultures that used the two alphabets—from philosophy to flora, food, and fauna—all in a winsome, anecdotal style. The section in *Alpha to Omega* on the Greek letter *rho* (Pρ), for example, explains by way of illustrating the word *rhetoric* that "a lesser known feature of the story [of Demosthenes, who was reputed to have learned to speak wonderfully by filling his mouth with pebbles and declaiming against the roar of the waves] is that [he] shaved off half his beard lest he be tempted to return to Athenian society before he had had plenty of time to complete these probably apocryphal oral calisthenics."

Word Mysteries and Histories

The subtitle of this book by the editors of the *American Heritage Dictionary* (Boston: Houghton-Mifflin, 1986) is *From Quiche to Humble Pie*, which gives some idea of its range. Like many books of the genre, it offers explanations of the origins of a selection of English words (selected according to principles apparent only to the editors, however) that are designed to delight and astound the reader. If you cannot live without knowing how *cannibal* got into English via Christopher Columbus and Mongol history, then this book is for you. Unlike most books of this kind, however, this one is beautifully illustrated and laid out. It is worth having for the way it looks as much as for what is in it.

Happy reading!

Lead Writing: Exploring the Underside

cott Rice is at it again, creating delight and groaning for all and sundry with his second collection of winning (?) entries from the Bulwer-Lytton Fiction Contest: *Son of "It Was a Dark and Stormy Night"* (New York: Penguin, 1986).

For those who have yet to learn of Professor Rice's off-duty enterprise, the Bulwer-Lytton Fiction Contest is an annual competition sponsored by San Jose State University, where Rice is on the English faculty. The competition challenges entrants to compose the worst possible opening sentence for a hypothetical novel. The contest perpetuates the name of Edward George Bulwer-Lytton, a Victorian novelist, whose *Paul Clifford* (1830) actually opens with what has become the time-honored lead for a hackneyed work of fiction (of late popularized by Snoopy): "It was a dark and stormy night."

Since 1983, the contest has attracted thousands of entries, each worse than the last. *Son of...* perpetuates the tradition established by its predecessor by offering up to the reading public such metaphorically excessive leads as

> As Roland slithered from a sly fox-trot into a torrid fandango, Melanie felt herself collapsing into his arms like a meringue, or maybe like a slightly warmed raspberry sauce, or no, she decided—definitely like a *pêche flambée*, but of course lit up on all the edges.

Metaphor Madness

For some leads, the issue is not so much blocking that metaphor as clawing one's way out of a regress of mind that threatens to become swampily infinite:

The hands of the little white porcelain clock, which had sat at her bedside since she was twelve years old and wildly in love with Baxton Heathley and which had been given to her by her Aunt Martha who had since died of a mysterious ailment in Peru while reportedly seeking information on the whereabouts of the famed black diamond which had belonged to her mother and her mother and her mother before her and so on down the line until it had disappeared during a hailstorm in Kansas where she was attending a convention of Astrologers Anonymous, crept slowly.

The Loaned Lead

Some leads, of course, are blatantly derivative. This one is attributed to a clone of C.S. Lewis but winds up sounding strangely like A.A. Milne:

Once there were five children whose names were Nigel, Agatha, Ian, Eudora, and Bruce, and this is the story about some perfectly splendid things that happened to them when they went away to live with Professor Edmund, a dear chap, who lived in a large house full of unexpected places with several servants named Mildred, Betty, Jeeves, and Brewster, but they did not have much to do with the story. [From *The Lynx, the Wizard, and the Chifforobe*]

Other leads are merely blatant:

Mary looked up from playing with the basket of kittens to hear her instructor repeat, "Remember, kitten in the left hand, skinning knife in the right!"

Read On

Some leave the reader breathless with anticipation:

Jack was going to be there in five minutes for dinner when Jill discovered she had baked her lipstick into the lasagne.

Still others predicate with unerring accuracy:

Bethune knew that his chances with Dimpled Elaine had diminished considerably the moment whatever it was fell from his nostril, uncurled, and scooted away.

Love Conquers All

Inevitably, the theme of many is love—often frustrated:

Ripping the third bodice from Belinda's hot, palpitating body, Lord Trewithit realized that he had also removed four camisoles, six petticoats, two corsets, and five pairs of pantaloons so far and there still seemed to be a lot of linen ahead, and with a cry of passion he demanded, "Good God, woman, are you nothing but skivvies?"

Bad lead writing can be, of course, as instructive as it is funny. Deliberately bad writing is even more so, since it magnifies, turning the blemish of the mediocre into an open wound. Rice's work more than amuses; it points us in a direction. As he says in his introduction to *Son of...*, "each sentence is a distilled work of literary criticism, a lampoon of various species of literary malpractice." And as such, these examples of bad lead writing should be not only enjoyed but studied.

Quick Fix

have yet to meet a writer or editor who was not at least mildly addicted to books on words. Fortunately, this craving is a minor social affliction and not too many babies are going unfed, although some mommies and daddies do have to be dragged out of the darkened recesses of a second-hand bookstore now and again.

If my own bookshelves are any indication, the deviant subculture to which we all belong has been transformed in our time into the victims of a minor publishing industry. Selections readily at hand range from the indispensable (H.W. Fowler, Wilson Follett, Stuart B. Flexner) to the frivolous (*Mrs. Byrne's Dictionary of Unusual, Obscure, and Preposterous Words,* by Josefa Byrne. Secaucus, NJ: Citadel Press, 1976); *Wordsmanship: Preposterously Long, Cruelly Obscure Substitutes for Common Everyday Words,* by Claurene DuGran. Old Lyme, CT: Verbatim Books, 1981).

One of the problems faced by those of us who buy these books is that the books tend to fall into two groups—the genuinely informative and the deliciously offbeat—without too much overlap. Books that ply the backwaters of words and usage while increasing one's useful knowledge of the language seldom appear between the same set of boards.

Public Service

But there is at least one such. It is by Bill Sherk, a professor at York University in Toronto: *500 Years of New Words* (out of print). Sherk provides two- to four-paragraph entries on the debuts of more than 450 words into English. Because the plan of the book is chronological, the reader can treat the book as diversionary reading, dipping into, say, the 17th century at will. Because it is based on a modicum of scholarship (mostly research in the *OED*), it can be used for genuine looking up. Because the book is well written, it is pleasurable either way.

Sherk provides a new word for every year from 1507 (*America*) to 1983 (*dermizip*). The alert reader will have quickly calculated that

1983 less 1507 yields fewer years than the promised 500. Sherk's response is eminently sensible: "We had to use [500 years] because a book called *476 Years of New Words* would not sell."

The totals are correct after the final chapter, "The Shape of Words to Come," which offers 25 new words that he predicts will enter the language by the year 2000.

Word lovers will find much to attract their attention and increase their enlightenment in this book. *Dictionary*, for example, turns out to have been used first (as something other than the title for a list of words) in 1526 as a reference to just such a word list; the first English dictionary, Sir Thomas Elyot's *Latin-English Dictionary*, appeared two years later. Early dictionaries were restricted to difficult words. Johnson's was the first all-inclusive English dictionary and has become known for its humor, as evidenced by the definition of a *window* as "an orifice in an edifice." A curiosity: The 1980 *Oxford American Dictionary* announces itself in a front-cover blurb as "the most authoritative paperbound dictionary," but does not include the word *paperbound*.

Lexicographer did not appear until 1658, and Sherk provides three thumbnail sketches of the giant lexicographers: Dr. Johnson, Noah Webster, and J.A.H. Murray.

Point and Tickle

The word *semicolon* (1644) provides Sherk with the opportunity to present a little punctuation history:

> ...a much earlier form of punctuation took the form of an upside-down semi-colon. It was called the point and tickle and it flourished in England between the ninth century and the twelfth. The point (.) was on the bottom; the tickle (') was on the top. According to Father Leonard Boyle, a specialist on ancient manuscripts and punctuation history, "The point and tickle developed when most reading was done aloud and the point signified a breathing space, but the tickle warned the reader not to change his tone of voice."

As possible additions to English in the remainder of the 20th century, Sherk offers the following: *deplasticate*—to rob someone of all credit cards; *leapian*—*a person whose birthday falls on February 29*; *vidience*—the proper term for a television audience; and *zeewyexical*—in reverse alphabetical order.

Unfortunately, Sherk offers no term for people who buy the kind of books he has written: *Logojunkie? Logofanat? Logobookisseur?*

And You Can Quote Me on That

ow that the quadrennial silly season is behind us, I guess we can hardly help noticing that—thanks to Senator Biden—quoting is back out of vogue. Lots of politicians like to pepper their speeches with quotes, especially those toiling at the long uphill climb from politico to statesman ("Politicians quote statesmen; statesmen quote their gardeners."—*Peter Sellers*). But they seem to be the only quoters around; and alas, the fondest desire of most remains not so much to quote as to be quoted.

Quotability is second nature to some, but seems to lie totally beyond the reach of others ("I never thought my speeches were too long; I've always enjoyed them."—*Hubert Humphrey*). Still others remain quotable no matter what ("Now when I bore people at parties, they think it's their fault."—*Henry Kissinger*).

Politicians aside ("I remain just one thing...a clown, and that places me on a higher plane than any politician."—*Charlie Chaplin*), you can still run into someone who quotes now and again if you hang out with college presidents, literary critics, or burned-out high-school Latin teachers. A favorite of mine was *"Ignis aurum probat, miseria fortes viros"* ("Fire tests gold, misery brave men."—*Seneca*). But I've had few opportunities to use it since 1956, the year I endured the misery of Latin II.

And that's the problem. What quoting gets you is mostly rolled eyeballs. I mean, who actually quotes in general conversation these days, besides George Will and William F. Buckley? Lots of people used to. It was a sort of conversational salt that teased out the flavor of tasty ideas ("I often quote myself; I find it adds spice to the conversation."—*George Bernard Shaw*). My Scotland-born grandfather spouted Bobby Burns whenever he could create the opportunity. The average churchgoer used to be able to punctuate any halfway interesting conversation with a verse of Scripture or an apt biblical metaphor, which, I may add, did not have to be explained to everyone in the room under 30 ("You can learn more about human nature by reading the Bible than by living in New York."—*William Lyon Phelps*).

But these days there seems to be a definite preference for Emerson's view ("Don't recite other people's opinions. Tell me what you know") over Montaigne's ("I quote others the better to express myself"). I am not sure where this aversion to other people's words comes from. Part of it, surely, is that people aren't nearly as well read as they used to be ("Since television, the well-read are being overtaken by the well-watched."—*Mortimer Adler*). Add to this the fact that much of what does get read doesn't bear repeating ("Jacqueline Susann is quite possibly the least quotable author of our era."—*Tazewell Pflaum*), and the beginnings of an explanation begin to take shape.

Still, I can't help wondering if we aren't the worse for letting our recapped recollections go flat. A quotation is, after all, a very versatile device. You can use one to be modest ("There's no trick to being a humorist when you have the whole government working for you."—*Will Rogers*), or to brag about the company you keep ("West Virginians have always had five friends—God Almighty, Sears Roebuck, Montgomery Ward, Carter's Little Liver Pills, and Robert C. Byrd."—*Sen. Robert C. Byrd*). You can quote to deliver an off-the-wall compliment ("There are a lot of mediocre judges and people and lawyers, and they are entitled to a little representation"—Sen. Roman Hruska on the nomination of G. Harold Carswell to the Supreme Court), or an insult ("He looks like a female llama who has just been surprised in her bath."—*Winston Churchill* on Charles de Gaulle).

The payoffs of quoting are subtle, but for those willing to invest in Bartlett's *Familiar Quotations* or Laurence J. Peter's *Peter's Quotations: Ideas for Our Time* (New York: Bantam Books, 1979), there are treasures indeed. At their best, quotations provide a serious talker with a triple whammy: authority ("Nothing overshadows truth so completely as authority."—*Alberti*); aptness ("A turn of phrase is as good as the turn of the screw."—*H. James*); and economy ("The moral majority is neither."—*B. Sticker*).

So, whether at the office ("Work is the refuge of people who have nothing better to do."—*Oscar Wilde*) or at play ("Golf is a good walk spoiled."—*Mark Twain*), let's start quoting again. But as we do, we need to recall the words of John Mason Brown: "A good conversationalist is not one who remembers what was said, but says what someone wants to remember."

Author's Warning: In a devilish mood, I have been known to make up quotes and attribute them to other people; a few of them are cited here.

An Editor's Glossary

rom time to time a letter comes pouring in from some distraught editor asking for an explanation of some editorial terms. Struggling out from under the weight of a #10 envelope the other day, we thought: "Enough! This situation is getting out of hand. Time for a glossary that will set the tyros straight on what all this mumbo-jumbo really means." We called on the shade of Ambrose Bierce, who obligingly left us with the following.

AAs—errors the editor should have prevented; also the chief source of income for printers

align—proofreader's mark meaning "the typesetter has the visual acuity of someone who uses Coke bottles for eyeglasses"

backed up—a printing mode that does not work on the paper you selected for this job (and you thought it was so attractive!)

bf—proofreader's mark meaning "make type bigger and fatter"

bleed—what your printing budget will do now that you have decided to run those four-color photos beyond the trim marks

bluelines—where typesetters hide their mistakes until after the job is printed

bullet—what the editor has to bite when an immovable deadline meets with an irresistible budget

cash flow—in the publications business, an oxymoron

casting off—a process for calculating the length of the shoehorn needed to slide 45 lines of typewritten copy into 7 typeset lines

column—a 42-inch vertical tabulation of statistics from which the decimal points and commas have mysteriously disappeared, and which now must be reset

contributor—someone who now wants his or her name set in type two points higher than on the galleys

copy—what you were working on but cannot now find; hint: Follow the coffee stain

"corrections, a couple of"—what the boss always wants to make just as the messenger arrives from the printer to pick up the *mechanicals (q.v.)*

draft—your reason for living, especially when preceded by the word *final*

editing—the process whereby the sow's ear of the copy you get is transformed into the silk purse of prose by your peerless ability to find and correct comma splices; in the *Writer's Glossary,* see *butchering my manuscript*

errata—flecks of spinach on the flashing editorial smile

freelancer—one who is late delivering a promised manuscript and then expects to be paid more because writing the article took so long

ghosting—the process of rendering idiots quotable

house style—the set of conventions that never makes any sense to the last person hired; thus, from that person's point of view, rules made to be broken

imprimatur—Latin for "I can't stand working on this any more. Send it to the printer!"

ISBN—a unique reference number given to every book; invented by a proofreader, the initials stand for either "I Should Be Nuts" or "I Stand By None (of this)"—no one is quite sure which

jargon—terms used by people whose writing you don't like

justification—spacing copy so that lots of weird-looking and irregular spaces appear between the words on each line; the first step in the generation of rivers

keyboarding—the work done by typists who make more than $18,000 a year

layout—editorial jargon for "a jigsaw puzzle in which one or more of the pieces does not fit"; as with jigsaws, the solution is trimming the edges off the pieces to fit the (news)hole

leading—in typeset copy, that which there is always either too much or too little of; leading, like type sizes, is measured in points and is pronounced to rhyme with "bedding," not "reading," unless we're talking about the gaol where Oscar Wilde spent some time, in which case it does rhyme with "Reading," but that's a different story altogether

ligature—a ligature is to letters of type as a ligament is to a set of bones; use of ligatures is falling out of favor, except among œnophiles, who like the way they look

list—comprises the new titles you have published this year (for which you have fond commercial hopes), as well as the backlist, which provides evidence to the contrary

list price—a negotiable figure attached to a book when it goes to market

manuscript—a cathexis; an object capable of provoking in the editor every emotional response ever catalogued by the psychiatric profession

margin—where to look to find the important information

mechanicals—where two percent of all editorial errors are discovered; unfortunately, this is the place they are most expensive to fix

orphan—together with widow, the single most frequent cause(s) of the passage of the word "damn!" from the lips of editors

pass for press—what to do when you can't stand it anymore

pe—in this glossary, an abbreviation for "printer's error"; in your printer's glossary, an abbreviation for "poor editing"

picture research—nobody's job, a fact undiscovered until press time

point—the unit for measuring the size of type, exactly 0.01383 inch in length; and to those who ask, "Why?" we say, "Why not?"

production manager—the mutterer with the vaguely disoriented expression, looking for the cream Danish

proofreader's marks—an idiosyncratic set of symbols used for correcting copy, of which everyone insists there is a standard version

ragged left/right/bottom—a way of arranging newsletter copy that no one is ever sure looks as good as it might if it were justified

recto—opposite of verso (*q.v.*)

review copies—(1) payola for college professors, literary critics, and young scholars on the make; (2) what line the bookshelves of assistant editors

runaround—(1) text set to fit around an illustration; (2) what you just got from the printer

scaling—a way of finding out there is no way you can get this picture to both look right and fit at the same time *separation*—a mysterious process required to print things in living color, controlled by a cartel that is making enough money to buy out Bloomingdale's

specifications—a minutely detailed description of the way a job is supposed to be done (see *air, castles in the*)

stock—the place in which your printer does not have any paper you absolutely have to have

typo—a mistake in the printed copy, always found by the boss on page 1 ten seconds after the job has been delivered from the printer

verso—opposite of recto (*q.v.*)

work in progress—in editing, alas, a tautology

An Editor's Venery: Or, a Synecdoche of Metaphors

lthough the dictionary defines *venery* as either the indulgence of sexual desire or the art or practice of hunting game, there is a much more exalted meaning to the term, invented by James Lipton, the author of *An Exaltation of Larks: The Venereal Game* (New York: Viking, 1968). Lipton adopted the term to describe a kind of word game; its object is to invent a striking phrase—poetic if possible, egregiously punsterish if necessary—to describe a collectivity. The trick of venery is to make an unexpected (and apt) noun out of some characteristic of whatever is to be collectivized ("a brawl of hockey players") or of the collectivity itself ("a cygnificance of swans").

Almost any area of endeavor is ripe for a round of venery ("a disputation of lawyers," "a haggling of accountants"), so why not editing? Herewith, then, a look at editing with a venereal eye. As with any infant science, however, there is a danger that zeal will overtake good sense and that some elements of our profession will be classified prematurely. What follows, therefore, is not a complete venery, but merely a hodgepodge of what we could think up as the deadline approached.

an amendment of copy editors	a substitution of pronouns
an abecdeary of indexers	a predication of verbs
a meticulation of proofreaders	an embellishment of adjectives
a drudge of lexicographers	a tempering of adverbs
a syllabation of orthographers	a yoke of conjunctions
a jeremiad of grammarians	a sprinkling of interjections

a composition of designers
a compulsion of editors
a hack of writers
an iteration of drafts
a backsliding of schedules
a pigtail of deletions
an alignment of margins
a transgression of errata
a loneliness of widows
a bereftment of orphans
a glossing of typos
a martyrdom of printers
an appellation of nouns

a specification of articles
a delimitation of prepositions
a stutter of hyphens
an exhibition of dashes
an elision of ellipses
a disjunction of semicolons
a clamor of exclamation points
a mooting of question marks
a terminus of periods
a throwaway of parentheses
an articulation of paragraphs
a completeness of sentences
a pendancy of participles

Your turn.

Hunting for Lost Positives

"Wattsa matta, ain'tcha got no couth?"

he question and its assumption—that *couth* in fact exists to cover what the speaker is after—raise for logophiles the flag of lost positives, words that some of us like to think might have once existed (as *couth* once did as the past participle of *can*), but which somewhere in their etymological peregrinations have shed their positive forms and come down to us only in the negative. ("Lost positives" are treated by William and Mary Morris, whose *Harper's Dictionary of Contemporary Usage* presents the only discussion of these words that I have found in standard works.)

A predilection for word-gaming carries with it the harmless right to hunt other such words as may be lurking in the language. According to the Morrises, seekers after lost positives have an honorable lineage, including the likes of columnist John Crosby, who once formed a Society for the Restoration of Lost Positives, and Bernice Fitz-Gibbon, a top advertising copywriter of a former era, who once handed in an ad encouraging young ladies to be "couth, kempt, and sheveled."

Having occasionally wondered myself about where all those lost positives have gone, and having a basic sympathy for lost causes akin to Crosby's, I set about trying to find a few. Armed only with a Webster's *New World* and an hour to kill, I went stalking. Taking my clue from the *un-* and *dis-* prefixes of Fitz-Gibbon's advertising trinity, I figured that negative prefixes would be the most fertile field. As it turned out, some were and some weren't.

Non-, for example, turned out to be pretty much of a bust, with two exceptions. *Descript* could be claimed as a found positive to express the idea of "well-defined," e.g., "George Hamilton is decidedly descript, sartorially speaking." And *plussed* begs to be instated as a word to mean a condition not of perplexity but of its near opposite, unflappability. It is the perfect word to describe Sir John Gielgud, for one, or whoever the current Archbishop of Canterbury might be.

Un- turned out to be equally sterile, with the aforementioned exceptions of *kempt* and *couth*. *Il-* also turned out to be a bust, with the exception of the possibilities in *lusion* as a found positive meaning a true conception, e.g., "Scroggins's lab assistant burst in shouting, 'Doctor! It's confirmed! Your hypothesis is a lusion!'"

Once I turned to *dis-*, things got a little more interesting. The prefix usually conveys the idea of "away and apart from" or, when used to form adjectives, of *not, un-*, or *the opposite of*. Here are a few found positives from *dis-* deserving consideration:

♦ *cern*—to recognize as belonging together, based on the notion that discern means to separate things mentally from one another, e.g., "I cern the Doobie Brothers, even though they are not really brothers."

♦ *parage*—to have esteem for, as in "It's easy to parage someone like Mother Teresa."

♦ *gruntled*—contented or complacent. Actually, James Thurber is credited with coming up with gruntled, and once wrote of his fellow staff members on the Paris *Herald Tribune* as "the most gruntled group I ever saw."

♦ *crepant*—in full agreement, e.g., "Phil and I are crepant on that."

♦ *combobulated*—having it all together, as in "Phylomina, though terrified, remained cool, calm, and combobulated."

♦ *criminatory*—having the tendency to dump things together, e.g., "Druscilla's wardrobe is utterly criminatory."

In- yielded up possibilities for *ert* as a coinage for wildly active; *ane* as a word to mean full of meaning; *sipid* as a fine synonym for zesty or flavorful; and the old standby *ept*, to mean dextrous. Ept's semantic cousin has already been found, but it's spelled *apt*.

Mal- offered only one found positive, namely *lign* (or *ign*), which could become a perfectly acceptable verb meaning to show goodwill ("We Redskins' fans should lign Cowboys' fans"). *Mis-* presented the possibility that a *creant* might become a new term for a nice guy, while *ogyny* bids fair to enter the language as the love of women.

Others pointed out by the Morrises include *defatigable* and *delible*, which actually showed up in a review by the respected drama critic of *The New York Times*, Clive Barnes, who wrote of one disappointing performer that "few have left so colorless and delible a memory in this role."

Doubtless there are others. Think of the possibilities. Not just for vocabulary enrichment or for the creation of nuance, but for advertising, PR, even poetry. Indeed, some pioneers have already blazed a trail there, or at least so say the Morrises, who reprint the following lines found on a bookstore bulletin board at Phillips Exeter Academy in the 1960s:

> I know a little man both ept and ert.
> An Intro? Extro? No, he's just a vert.
> Sheveled and couth and kempt, pecunious, ane:
> His image trudes on the ceptive brain.

Advertently yours.

The Portable Curmudgeon

mong my favorite figures in the editorial pantheon is the cigar-chomping, hard-bitten, bourbon-belting, crusty, irascible, iconoclastic city-room tyrant. This is the misanthrope whose view of human nature is so cynical that he would sooner submit to an evening at the opera than so much as lift an eyebrow when his neighbor, a loving husband and Episcopal rector, becomes an ax murderer one morning, dismembering his devoted wife of 30 years for coddling the eggs too long. His only question would be, "What took him so long?" This is Lou Grant as an H.L. Mencken knock-off—the world-class curmudgeon.

What curmudgeons have long lacked is a manual—a handbook to tuck in the pockets of their hair shirts for ready reference in time of pique. No more. Browsing the bookstores the other day I came across *The Portable Curmudgeon,* compiled and edited by Jon Winokur (New York: New American Library, 1987). This book is all the ammunition the aspiring churl will ever need for gunning down the latest hypocrisy or pretense. The book is 300 pages of alphabetically arranged pet peeves, from Abstract Art ("A product of the untalented sold by the unprincipled to the utterly bewildered"— Al Capp) to Youth ("The denunciation of young people is a necessary part of the hygiene of older people and greatly assists in the circulation of the blood"—Logan Pearsall Smith).

The quotes from all over are great, but the book's real treasures are the brief anecdotal collections from some of the world's great curmudgeons:

♦ Mencken (of course), who once described his life's work as "stirring up the animals" and his editorial philosophy at *The Smart Set* as "nothing uplifting"

♦ W.C. Fields, who, when a friend caught him reading the Bible in a hospital bed during his last illness, explained that he was "just looking for loopholes"

♦ George S. Kaufman, who once asked a monopolistic conversation partner at dinner, "Madam, don't you have any unexpressed thoughts?"

♦ The truly razor-tongued Dorothy Parker, who, when told that Clare Boothe Luce was always kind to her inferiors, replied, "Where does she find them?"

In reading *The Portable Curmudgeon,* I realized that I don't know very many editors, if any, who have what you would call a sweet disposition. I called a few of them to check this out and was mostly rewarded with either "Are you crazy? In this business?" or "Don't you have anything better to do than bother me? Get a job!"

That pretty much covers it. Editors are drawn to the curmudgeonly way of life, I think, because it suits not their personalities but the profession. And like teetotaling, curmudgeoning can't be done in secret. Editors get that way because they are mostly paid skeptics. They are in the business of assuming that there is something wrong with what they're looking at, and it is their job to find it. They see too much pomposity, hypocrisy, and double-dealing to remain trusting—or sweet-tempered—for long. Their only real masters, the clock and calendar, are absolutely heartless, and the editors respond in kind.

Becoming a curmudgeon is simply a way of coping, a way of making the editorial bed of thorns a little easier to lie on. And, as Jon Winokur's collection seems to be telling us, if you can do it in a way that makes other people smile—or wince—with you, then maybe you've somehow kept your humanity intact.

Editorial Experts, Inc. (EEI), is a full-service publications consulting firm based in Alexandria, VA. EEI's services include writing, editing, proofreading, word and data processing, design and graphics, abstracting, indexing, workshops for publications professionals, and temporary and permanent placement in the publications field. EEI plans and manages conferences and produces the publications arising from them. EEI also publishes the award-winning *Editorial Eye* newsletter and books in the editorial and publications field. For more information on EEI's professional books and seminars, write to Editorial Experts, Inc., 85 S. Bragg St., Ste. 400, Alexandria, VA 22312.